PSYCHOTHERAPY AND RELIGION

PSYCHOTHERAPY
AND
RELIGION

JOSEF RUDIN

TRANSLATED BY
ELISABETH REINECKE AND
PAUL C. BAILEY, C.S.C.

UNIVERSITY OF NOTRE DAME PRESS
NOTRE DAME   LONDON

Published as PSYCHOTHERAPIE UND RELIGION,
© 1960 by Walter-Verlag, Olten and Freiburg in Breisgau.
Second edition published in 1964.

Excerpts from *Answer to Job* by C. G. Jung used with the permission of
Bollingen Foundation Inc., New York, and
Routledge & Kegan Paul Ltd., London

LIBRARY OF CONGRESS CATALOG CARD NUMBER: 68-12291
MANUFACTURED IN THE UNITED STATES OF AMERICA

CONTENTS

Foreword to the First Edition

The publication of this work is not intended primarily for a narrow circle of professionals (even though some points in it may, we hope, stir the representatives of modern depth psychology to take a position). Rather, it is directed to the wider circle of those who are alarmed by the real or apparent opposition between the new insights of depth psychology, resulting from the investigations of the unconscious and its lawfulness, and the basic convictions of theology, especially of moral theology. To go even further, we would like to address all those who are open to a problem that necessarily arouses the inner realm of the psyche, in that it intensely activates this realm and widens it beyond all expected measure. Assurances provided by a mere illumination of consciousness seem inevitably too weak in this matter, for, as we know, the energy-stream which rises out of the wellsprings of the unconscious and the nature-given life-dynamic demands stronger safety valves. It is man who is viewed and questioned here in a new and hitherto not so completely recognized totality.

The external format of the book is according to usual scientific procedure: statement of the problem, demonstration of the psychic manifestations, disclosure of the backgrounds and connections, attempts at clarification and position taking. However, the internal form, which, hopefully, is transparent through all these essays, is that of dialogue, a conversation seeking clarity. In this conversation the one who, as the youngest, talks the most and works hardest to make himself intelligible is the representative of analytical depth psychology and of the psychotherapy founded thereon. The other partners in the conversation come from sectors of the philosophy of culture, education, and, lastly yet more and more to the fore, from the realm of theology. Thus the dialogue proceeds, so to speak, in two phases—both of which, in their final and deepest meaning, have the same goal: the image of man, seeking its authentic gestalt first on the natural plane and yet, in so doing, almost as a foregone conclusion trying to reach a higher level. The first phase is aimed at the structure of the person, in that initially it emphasizes a more conscious recognition of the soul and its developmental tendencies, and then, by way of the many steps of individual life-formation and of a systematic widening of the inner realm of freedom, it approaches the structure-given goal of being-person. The second phase purposes to see, on the person-level that has been achieved, a more vital confrontation with the at first immanently revolving God-image, to specify in this confrontation the lurking dangers of neurotic perfectionism, and to point out that nature-grounded attitude which aims at an authentic transcendence.

Even though this book is an assemblage of the past seven years and does not strive for systematic unity, an inner spiraling movement should be noticeable in which problems repeatedly meet one another, interconnect, and display always new aspects beyond those already illuminated. An honest outline of the many-layered problem areas seemed more important to me than the anticipation of final answers, for which the time does not yet appear to be ripe.

Zurich, February, 1960.

Dr. Josef Rudin

Foreword to the Second Edition

In the second edition, the chapter "Psychology as a Way to Religion" has been replaced by a discussion of "Religious Experience in the Conscious and Unconscious." It should help to provide a more unified view of the depth psychological character of this book. A letter of C. G. Jung, written after the first publication of the book, has also been incorporated; it contains some thoughts of this great pioneer of analytical psychology in regard to the problems of "psychotherapy and religion." We hope that this second edition will be received with the same enthusiasm as the first.

Letter of Professor C. G. Jung to the Author

Dear Doctor:

I have just finished your book, which I read from begin-ning to end with the greatest interest, for I have always been intent on building—or at least attempting to build—a bridge between the two disciplines that are concerned with the cura animarum, namely, theology on the one hand and clinical psychology on the other. In spite of their different points of departure, they meet each other in the empirical soul of the human person. On the Protestant side my attempts found fruit in Professor Hans Schär of Bern; on the Catholic, you have successfully circumnavigated the rocks of theoretical knowledge and therefore have given psychology a living space in the sphere of Catholic spirituality—in praiseworthy contrast to Anglo-Saxon and French theologians who are even unaware that theoretical knowledge is problematic and hence deny empirical psychology the right of existence. It is the merit of your work, which cannot be highly enough appreciated, that it enables us to go a great part of the way together, and, as is my hope, to the benefit of both of us. We are both convinced that our perilous times are in great need of psychological enlightenment and that someone must make a start, which, however, cannot be made alone. Thus, not only in my regard but above all for the project itself, your positive position is a great encouragement and an important step forward.

The difference in our points of departure as well as those of our clients and their spiritual needs requires an "external" difference in our aims. Your theological orientation is accommodated to the axes of your ecclesiastical realm, while I feel obliged to follow the unpredictable lines of the way of individuation and its symbolism; in other words, while you speak in a more definite way about Christ, I, as a mere empiricist, must cautiously use the term ἄνθρωπος, since this term has a more than five-millennia-old, more or less conscious, phenomenological history as an archetype. This term is more indefinite in idea and thus more apt for use. As it stands, I am working mainly with people who have either lost or never possessed their Christian character or else profess other religions while still belonging to the human family. I cannot rest content with the opinion of a theologian friend of mine who said: "The Buddhists are no concern of ours." In the consultation room of the physician they certainly are our concern, and they deserve to be spoken to in a universal human language.

Thus I well understand that, from your approach, the process of individuation does not receive the same prominence in your discussions as it does in mine.

One more question: Is there a hint of reproach (on the occasion of the Answer to Job) in your statement that I have not taken "biblical theology" into consideration. If

I had, I would have written from the theological stand-point, and you would be correct in charging me with blasphemy. In Protestant circles I was likewise reproached for neglecting the higher criticism. Why did these gentlemen not publish a book of Job that fitted the demands of their own opinions? I am a layman and have access only to the (translated) Job in the way it is served to the lay-public cum consensu autoritatis. Yet, it is this Job that the layman reflects on and not the speculations of textual criticism which he has never encountered and which also make no relevant contribution to the spirit of this book.

These remarks are just by the way. I am truly happy to find so much to agree with in your book, which, I hope, will attract a great many readers.

Sincerely yours,
C. G. Jung

Küsnacht/Zurich
April 30, 1960

PART ONE

CHAPTER I

The Normal Man

NONCOMMITTAL REFLECTIONS ON A MUCH ABUSED CONCEPT[1]

I A SKIRMISH

For the *statistician* the normal man is one who closely
approaches the mean value of a theoretically infinite dis-
tribution of digits. He is a normal consumer of ordinary commodities, requires an exact number of calories,
works eight hours a day and sleeps the same. He drinks
forty quarts of beer a year and goes bowling once a week,
unless he would rather play poker. He marries between
the ages of twenty and thirty and has two children. He
has a life insurance policy, is a willing yet not overzealous
taxpayer and dies at about the age of sixty-five.

The *popularizing, Sunday-supplement* psychologist

---

[1] These "reflections" are not intended to enter into the discussion regarding the philosophical concept of norm as a concept of ethics and values,
as did Hans Kunz in 1954 in *Psyche* (VIII, 5/6). Rather, we are speaking here about the thoughtless use of the concept "normal" found not
only in everyday life but very often also in psychological expositions.

3

highly esteems as normal the man who lives a healthy sex life with only trivial escapades, abstains from overindulgence in alcohol, prefers a pipe to cigarettes, is not enamored of way-out art, but certainly has a hobby. This normal man does not sink into long-lasting depressions —why should he? He has life efficiency because he is adaptable.

From the viewpoint of the *sociologist*, the normal man is the man on the street who has a middle-class income (and tax exemptions according to the number of his children). He lives in a housing development, is a union member, belongs to an association for leisure-time activity, subscribes to a daily newspaper and one magazine, is insured against accident and unemployment, and is a member of about three clubs.

The *advertising profession* is very well acquainted with the normal man: His average reactions, his urges and needs, both conscious and unconscious, have been analyzed and measured. Whether selling toothpaste, stockings, cigarettes, or refrigerators, soda pop, watches, soap, or pencils, a well-proportioned female is always provided to act as stimulant for the product advertised.

Fashion designers, movie producers, and preachers of morals see the normal man as a victim of his drives, incessantly and cunningly releasing, greedily expecting, and automatically responding to—sex appeal. For *chefs* and *restaurant owners* the normal man is a lover of steaks with baked potatoes and a salad, followed by pie a la mode, and so forth.

The *normal man* himself sees the normal man as the

one who always fits into the picture. He need not consult a psychotherapist, since at all times he displays well-ordered behavior. He relaxes in a well-calloused, scar-covered conscience. His main concern is not to be abnormal, not to be conspicuous, not to be noticed, and in no case ever to reveal his bank account. The normal man gives everyone his due: the state, the church, his wife, and the manufacturers of shaving cream. The normal man is a model for statisticians, Kinsey psychologists, bureaucrats, and sociologists looking for work. Tell me how your normal man looks and I will tell you who you are!

II TO THE POINT

The problem of normality immediately reveals a multiplicity of aspects when we ask who is actually competent to establish valid standards by which we can judge, in the concrete case, who is normal and who abnormal. At least four very dedicated and competent groups are concerned with this question.

The *biological-medical* scientist will speak authoritatively only in respect to the normality of body structure and of the vegetative-sensitive nervous system, but in doing so he is already making very important statements regarding the normality of the whole man. The biological-physiological structure and its extremely complex functionality (think only of the hormonal functions) are, as we know, fundamentally connected with psycho-spiritual behavior and influence it either in a normal or a pathologizing way. This being the case, the judgment regarding biological-physiological normality is no longer confined to this area but points far beyond it into the psycho-spiritual realm. The old saying *"mens sana in corpore sano"* takes on new significance when we call to mind how much its conceptual content has increased and how new psychosomatic investigations are constantly expanding and deepening its meaning. True enough, we also hear that at times a fiery spirit works in a weak body and that outstanding geniuses have struggled through their whole life with somatic inadequacies. But these are noted as exceptions for the very reason that normally it is the other way around. Not infrequently, in spite of their excellent productivity, geniuses with a sick bios display a spirituality which through its radicalism, exaggerations, extreme sharpness and intolerance reveals itself as a typical and generally unpleasing overcompensation.[2] Hence, the judgment of normality-abnormality cannot neglect the medical-biological viewpoint.

Psychology, especially test psychology and depth psychology, values the normality of the psychic function-apparatus and its individual powers and potentialities, as well as the adaptation of active and passive behavior. This results in essential judgments concerning psychic balance or imbalance (caused, for instance, by unconscious, neuroticizing complexes). The layman often rashly

---

[2] Cf. Lange-Eichbaum, *Genie, Irrsinn und Ruhm* (1956). Even though this pathology of genius should on many points be referred to very cautiously, one cannot ignore the overwhelming accumulations of pathographic material.

reproaches psychological investigation and methods of treatment for a generalizing panpathologism. Granted, even the cool and critical psychologist is subject to *deformation professionnelle*, but can any profession exempt itself from this?

Depth psychology rightly points out that in everyday life the neurotic often cannot be distinguished from the healthy "normal man." The neurotic may be quite efficient in his profession, occupy a high position as politician, teacher, researcher, artist, or preacher, and at first sight be judged by his environment as very "normal." Yet this does not mean that, in some barely accessible sector of his psyche, he may not be the victim of a compulsion of a fear complex. In a juridical sense, he may be labelled as quite "efficient in business," even though he is poisoning and destroying his marriage in its very foundations through strange inhibitions or a total lack of inhibition. Shall we, therefore, call him "normal," simply because his business associates or even his closest relatives have no suspicion of this complex? A person can be fully responsible for a sexual offense and perhaps only thirty per cent responsible for a theft, and vice versa. But such a complex may someday have a tremendous influence on his public behavior and can, for instance in the case of a politician, lead to decisions which cause national catastrophes.[3]

Thus the doctrine of psychic complexes demands necessary differentiations even within the sphere of the

---

[3] It may be mentioned here that, especially since World War II, attempts to develop a "psychology of politics" are increasing.

normal. Normality no longer appears to be an across-the-board concept which, based on superficial knowledge, can be worn as a ready-made etiquette, just as the concept of abnormality should never be applied simply in a generalized sense. Could not the principle *bonum ex integra causa, malum ex quocumque defectu* perhaps be taken as permission for a kind of general skepticism regarding normality? The trained eye of the physician and of the conscientious psychotherapist observes easily and unmistakably certain deviations from what he considers normal. Should these observations, therefore, be rejected as panpathologizing, or do they not prove the fact that the truly and completely normal does not exist? (It is obvious that here "normal" is no longer the popular concept but is applied in a more precise sense.) The goal of psychotherapy is not at all the "normal man" as understood, for instance, by the man on the street; neither is it what is commonly called "happiness," or even so-called "effective living" or "social adaptation," as it was in the beginnings of psychoanalysis. "The goal of psychotherapy is not to bring the patient into an impossible state of happiness but to provide him strength and philosophical patience to endure suffering."[4] Thus, from the psychological and, above all, the psychotherapeutic standpoint, the concept of normal has been divested of many a naïve notion and is a far cry from the popular conception.

In view of the fact that empirical sciences make every

[4] C. G. Jung, *The Practice of Psychotherapy* (*Collected Works*, Bollingen Series XX [New York: Pantheon] vol. 16, 1954) 81.

effort to point out the great complexity of the concept of normality and consequently insist on the use of this term in a responsible sense, we must ask to what degree *anthropological philosophy* participates in this development. Anthropological philosophy surveys the normal man generally according to what it considers to be the "nature" of man and, abstracting from concrete expressions, seeks through physiological and psychic given states to find the normal man where this nature appears relatively pure in its specificity and wholeness. It is above all the "essence" philosophers who hold to this idea of man and somehow see nature as an effective principle of entelechy. The three basic positions which have been considered possible are well-known: One can see the nature of man only in its spiritual dimensions and its freedom or, equally one-sidedly, only in its subjection to and amalgamation with matter. Or else one sees spirit and matter as natural components fusing in some way or another into a human *compositum*. This can lead to spiritualistic-idealistic, materialistic, and synthetic (hylomorphic, for instance) concepts of the normal man.

For example, we can have before us a normal man who in the overemphasis of his spirit-freedom does not want to accept the manifold limitations of his body and spacial-temporal factors, who is convinced that every illness can be cured by spiritual energies, who despises every natural instinct as subhuman ("abnormal") and plays the angel, or who, in a complete turnabout, considers these instincts irrelevant, like a nutrition drive, and completely indulges in them. (We are reminded of certain Orphics and gnostic groups or of the quietist groups of the Middle Ages.) Or we may meet the type who considers himself as the most highly developed mammal, which has attained special forms of social life but which cannot escape the fate of matter's decay and its constant transformation. Therefore he consciously sides with matter and praises a corresponding way of existence. Finally, we confront a human being who, in an extremely complex interlacement of matter, instinct, and spirit, is supposed to bring to realization a novel and independent being who is characterized by the tormenting tensions and polarities which cause suffering and misery but also ever new upswings.

Today there is opposition to these very static concepts of man from all those who cannot circumscribe the multilayered riches and the creative spontaneity of man by a meager abstraction and who therefore do not view normal man as an essence poured millions of times into the bottle of an incidental phenotype. They refuse to ignore the individual historical situation that cooperates always in a singular way in the concrete formation of man and causes the realm of his individual freedom to be greater or lesser. Here man experiences something of his inexchangeable uniqueness and loneliness, and the talk about "the normal man" becomes balderdash pushing man into unauthenticity. The historical dimension and the individual situation must be incorporated in the concept of normal. For instance, we can no longer consider primitive, cannibalistic tribes as normal, even though their cannibalism is a part of their religious cult. Similarly, for the citizens of the nineteenth century the idea of being a slave was incompatible with the concept of normal existence: "To be man means to be free"; while for primitive Christianity the words of St. Paul were still valid: "Wast thou a slave when called? Let it not trouble thee" (1 Cor. 7:21). It would be fascinating to follow the changes in the concept of the normal man through the individual historical epochs and find it confirmed that man in his innermost depth is a temporal being, a being of manifold historical determination. Thus, even the speculations of philosophers indicate that the problem of the normal man is multifaceted and an ever new question.

But is it possible that the *theological* view, based on Christian faith, has the final answer to this question? I admit that the Christian image of man is neither the empirical image of our sciences nor is it identical with what human wisdom in the course of ages has learned about man and organized into profound systems. Rather, we must consult the revelation of God, where, as we know, very early the decisive statement is made that God created man according to his image and parable. Thus, this image-ness and parable-ness of man are, from the theological point of view, the norm of man's normality. According to the opinion of theologians, however, this image was quickly spoiled and reduced. Then, is fallen man, in the state of original sin, no longer a normal man? The answer to this question depends largely on whether one advocates Lutheran and Calvinistic concepts of original sin or whether he agrees with the Catholic doctrine that original sin did not at all radically corrupt man—in spite of seriously weakening him and separating him from the sphere of grace and friendship of God, it did not destroy his innermost nature. Nevertheless, the extent of this loss and weakening led Christ to say: "Amen, amen, I say to thee, unless a man be born again, he cannot see the kingdom of God" (John 3:3). But, viewed theologically, is one who is not reborn a normal man? Is he not, rather, a distortion, a caricature of the image which God himself had in mind? Could one not rightly agree with the statement that Christ is the only normal man? Consequently, would not the saints be those most likely to be on the way to normality? Those very saints, in other words, whose biological-physiological potential was seldom remarkable and whose psychic balance often was achieved only at the end of a long, painful struggle? This theological view, which we merely allude to here, proves to be just as problematical as the view of the profane sciences and of philosophy.

In the course of this discussion, perhaps we have gradually become distrustful and wary. Does normality and the normal man exist at all? Would it not be wise to eliminate this vague concept and replace it by an exact characteristic? Or are we so set on this illusion of the normal that we maintain the normality of a man should never be questioned until the contrary is clearly proved? Yet, the use of the word *normal* cannot be suspended, for we all have a deep-seated need of making comparisons and therefore of having a norm, and most people are subject to the prejudice that they ought to make value judgments concerning their fellowmen. But our "noncommital reflections" may perhaps encourage greater differentiation and more mature standards. Finally, is it not the "others," the "outsiders," the "unadapted geniuses" to whom mankind owes its greatest discoveries, scientific inventions, and works of art? To these outsiders "normal men" are generally too boring and contemptible, are mere serial products of nature, without their own faces. And yet, what if human society consisted only of outsiders? How great would our longing be for the tiresome "normal man"!

CHAPTER II

Soul-Anxiety

AN UNADMITTED PROBLEM

Not only among philosophers of culture but also in broader areas, anxiety today is considered an "existential" of human existence, the innermost expression of the situation in which man finds himself. This anxiety is something irrational and should not be confused with the fear of definite, concrete dangers. Rather, it is a feeling, lurking in the depth of the being, that does not quite know its provocators, and even less has any idea of where to look for them. This radical anxiety has been the mysterious companion of mankind since the beginning. We are aware of the eruptions of anxiety among primitive tribes, of the sudden collective panic that overcomes them apoplectically, and of their more or less successful attempts to find anxiety-screening practices and anxiety-freeing rituals. Compulsive anxiety-driven ideas are calmed by equally compulsive magical customs and at times are transformed into enthusiastic outbursts of joy and wildly ecstatic orgies. In early stages of development, the collectivity, with its rules and prohibitions, channels

15

and directs anxiety-awakening and anxiety-liberating experiences. In more enlightened and science-oriented epochs, feelings of anxiety become more articulated through reason, transformed into controllable fear, and very many anxiety-causing factors are "demythologized." Knowledge, discoveries, research in the areas of biology, medicine, chemistry, and physics help overcome many dangers and reduce the number of threats to a minimum. Then the deeper existential anxiety must retire to a few remaining positions, and it even seems to be driven back so far that one begins to hope it could one day be completely eliminated from our existence. Or is such a hope but a naïve illusion, since one has no idea of the undergrounds of the soul? Is anxiety always only more deeply submerged into the unconscious and there dammed up so that it must intensify to the maximum its irrational character? And will it not, then, according to the law of enantiodromia (*les extrêmes se touchent*), suddenly break out and violently force its way into our consciousness, producing there strange phenomena of anxiety?[1] Our time's neurosis epidemic confirms that this breakthrough has taken place and is continuing to take place, since disproportionate, irrational anxiety is a typical sign of every serious neurosis.

If anxiety belongs to the nature of man as a "basic condition,"[2] it is man's ethical task to keep an eye on its

[1] This "law" goes back to Heraclitus. In modern psychology, C. G. Jung has especially emphasized it in its comprehensive meaning. In this connection we may call to mind the phenomena of "flying saucers," also interpreted by Jung as psychic phenomena.
[2] From the theological viewpoint we can allude here to the state of man's fallenness; existential anxiety can be understood as its consequence.

water level and carefully supervise its underground channels with their sudden rises and possibilities of hidden
drainage. To do so we must know more about the basic
forms of anxiety and their significance. Fear of death is
recognized as one of these basic forms and this makes
possible the many attempts to deal meaningfully with
the problem of death.[3] We would like here to venture the
statement that there is another basic form of anxiety,
almost equally important, which should more consciously
be grasped and formed. This is the fear of one's own soul
and its depths, of the soul's dark labyrinth and its hiding places which everyone has within himself. For a
meaningful working out and a more conscious endurance
of this anxiety, the sense of ethical responsibility must
still be awakened and, even prior to this, conditions
must be made favorable through a better knowledge of
the soul.

Our statement that modern man suffers from a latent,
disproportionate fear of his own soul may at first sight
seem absurd. With a smile we are referred to the flood
of psychology conventions, courses, lectures, books, and
articles. Was there ever a time so intensively concerned
about the soul as ours? After all, we are the first to create
the special professions of the clinical psychologist and
psychotherapist. In all kinds of psychological institutes
new insights are methodically worked out and systematically deepened. Already here and there a creeping fear

[3] Cf., for instance: Karl Rahner, *On the Theology of Death* (Freiburg:
Herder, 1961); also: Ladislaus Boros, *The Mystery of Death* (New York:
Herder & Herder, 1965).

of this army of psychologists is beginning. "Help me, I am being tested!" a wit wrote recently. Interest in occult parapsychological phenomena, in manifestations such as clairvoyance, telepathy, etc., has also been awakened. In fact, there has probably never been a time that so overtly, without any blinds and with scientific exactitude, has sought to reveal the abysses of the soul. Can we say, then, that this era is afraid of the soul?

Perhaps this grandiose display concerning the soul is the very confirmation of our statement, since it is possible that in certain instances psychology itself, so correct and cunning in its attempts to unmask the soul, actually becomes a curtain before it. Often, perhaps, we try (unconsciously) to scientifically domesticate, to render harmless and ineffective, a force that should be the alarmer, since it sets up an allergic resistence to our purpose-oriented and technological interpretation of existence and could make us "unfit for life." It is even open to question whether the former practices of using magic and ritual celebrations to screen oneself from the power of irrational soul-anxieties might not have been more adequate than our own efforts to deliniate the possibilities and limits of the soul with dozens of tests in order to bring it into a well-ordered, coordinated system. Here the intellect has certainly invented some subtle moves— the *homo ludens* has made remarkable progress—but the moves of the soul are even more tricky and impermeable, and many of its inventions cannot be registered by any psychological seismograph.

The intellectual-spiritual processes are more easily traced and the refined expression-possibilities of the body more sensitively coexperienced than many psychic events which take place in the underground, scarcely noticeable to the subject. Are we, then, not justified in fearing a power that lives and works quietly and inconspicuously, building its roads and establishing a warehouse not only of valuable goods but also of powerful explosives? Great feats of intellect cannot be exhibited fast enough on the market of culture. They are offered with a precise label, and physical education, too, is practiced according to testable methods. Only the soul with its powers, with its immeasurable realm of imagination, feeling, and moods, finally escapes every psychological computer system and every top-qualified electronic machine. Unknown and unrecognized it traces and retraces its own labyrinthian ways. Should we not rightly fear this unknown that wanders through the rooms of our house, living on our provisions and perhaps impudently sitting on gasoline drums playing with matches? Perhaps we should look further into the many forms of this unadmitted fear of the soul. The more clearly we see them, the more they can be freed of their excessive intensity and brought back to the degree of anxiety that is given us along with our nature and in which form it does not lead to illness but is beneficial by its very acceptance.

FORMS OF SOUL-ANXIETY

The Indirect Form: Fear of Psychology

Today we first meet soul-anxiety indirectly, and almost in passing, as *fear of psychology*. Whoever goes to the psychologist for the first time has the unpleasant sensation that psychologists are people of mystery. Do their X-ray eyes not penetrate into our unconscious sexual tendencies, our concealed perverse inclinations, or our disproportionate urges toward self-assertion, and relentlessly unveil them? Complexes repressed for years are shoved into the daylight of consciousness, and even those unworthy urges which have been carefully hidden from one's own ego are placed before the eyes of this ego as irrefutable facts; on the other hand, all noble behavior and assiduously practiced virtues are peremptorily checked with a black question mark. Should we not have a sense of fear and strong discomfort in the face of an analysis that does not fail to notice those affectionately pampered little self-deceits which for some (possibly many) are their life's happiness? Or when the fine-spun fabric of the great life-lie is more and more punched full of holes?

"That which makes a science of the soul so difficult is not the soul but the masquerade of the soul which the will to power has moved between the soul and the observer. Thus he who, removing all masks, would have succeeded only in arriving at the soul would have by far the greater part of his investigation of the science of character already behind him" (Klages).

We understand how the restless anxiety concerning psychology is an insecurity regarding the condition of one's own soul, even if this anxiety tries to camouflage itself with jokes and anecdotes about psychologists. But fear of psychology can also have deeper motives. There are many testing methods and various schools of soul analysis, each arguing in defense of its own experience and insights. What method and school can one trust in such delicate matters? Are we not perhaps merely at the mercy of experiments which are reasonably abhorred? The answer to this question is imperative. In our opinion it is definitively wrong and disastrous if—because of theoretical counterpositions which at times are exaggerated by the very ones concerned (take, for example, the interpretation of neurosis)—the great common factors and concordances are overlooked and the more or less important but irrefutable successes of many analyses are not recognized. Modern-day psychology cannot afford, as did that of the nineteenth century, to bypass the pressing current questions concerning the soul and to lock itself up in a laboratory of apparatus in order to conduct experiments emulating those of chemistry and physics. Psychology cautiously enters into life, into the uninterrupted process of the individual soul, into its ups and downs, pouring light into its secret desires and longings, its true or seeming failures, loosening its anxieties and compulsive ideas, supporting its development and patiently enduring relapses. It is almost impossible for a third person to fully participate in such psychic development and guidance. Therefore psychology should not shy away from misunderstandings and must reckon with accusations of heresy.[4]

Not infrequently fear of psychology is needlessly inten-

---

[4] Although there is a "technique" of analysis that can be learned and the beginning analyst must have his "cases" examined by an instructor-analyst, it is obvious that by such procedure only the more flagrant errors and deficiencies of an analysis can be avoided.

sified because other sciences all too hastily reject methods or well-founded results of analytical psychology. It has taken a long time for the irrefutable facts established by depth psychology to be accepted. The term *psychologism* is a little too brashly sloganized and betrays a suspicious helplessness. Also, a reserve and fearfulness, which is probably only psychologically understandable, often characterizes one who reads psychological books and writings always through metaphysical spectacles. This attitude ordinarily leads to a shifting of the point in question, thus instigating premature and unnecessary opposition. Certainly all human assertions have a background which makes it possible for them to be ordered into a final context and to be interpreted in a total attitude toward all manifestations of existence. But the intent of most psychological theories is primarily only a more precise and penetrating description of psychic events and an interpretation based on the contexts and goals of the soul's fields of force (that is, based on second-last "causes"). Therefore they have heuristic value and can be meaningful and important.

Another difficulty is that this newly discovered realm of the soul must be expressed in an already established vocabulary, although some of these concepts can also have a philosophical meaning. Should psychology create a completely new language of concepts—as has already been attempted—which would then remain unintelligible not only to the man on the street but also to vast academic circles? No doubt there would be some advantage in passing on scientific insights that are coded primarily for the initiated, thus protecting these insights from misinterpretations and misuse. But the disadvantages of such a cipher-code would be equally great and only intensify the fear of psychology. Moreover, a secret science almost necessarily isolates itself from contact with concrete life and is in danger of getting lost in little side streets or of becoming esoteric, which again would only increase the anxiety over such a science of the soul.

Direct Forms: Resistance—Fixation—Escape

The fear of one's soul, however, is often manifested also in a very direct and clear way. Even in the beginnings of the analysis the well-known phenomenon of "resistance" is discovered and thoroughly investigated. This resistance comes up almost invariably whenever a new stage of individual development is demanded. Every such step is a risk and a yielding up of the present absolute standpoint, and it demands as much courage as patience. It is a descent into the depth of the unconscious, which at first is experienced only as a dark, undulating chaos. This is a place to fear and avoid, this depth where darkling forces, emotions, and vital stirrings rule. In this place dwell powers which are only intimated, which one does not admit to himself often for his entire life and which are therefore projected toward the outside into political, religious, social, or scientific enemies, into Jews, Freemasons and Jesuits.

But giving up the present condition means a loosening of ties that are often tenaciously held and which are basically hindering: the unhealthy parental ties (of reciprocal nature) are the best known example. We deal here with a basic law of all psychic unfolding and development, which is also emphasized in the ascesis of almost all religions: "Leave your country." The great inner freedom, so praised as the goal of personality development, makes such mighty demands that only a few can actually achieve and maintain it. "There has never been anything more difficult for the individual as well as for the entire human race to endure than this very freedom" (Dostoevski, "The Grand Inquisitor" in *The Brothers Karamazov*). As a result of this insight, analysis will, varying according to the circumstances, content itself with an alleviation of the pathological symptoms and a better adjustment to the environment, or else it will attempt to initiate the great process of individuation which can lead the person to authenticity. It should not now surprise us that in both cases, however, an inner tension shows up and that fearful crises have to be endured, since the fixations that are to be broken not only have had a hindering effect and have often led to very severe organic and psychic neuroses, but they also have become quite comfortable and even profitable. These fixations can take on many different forms. The danger of remaining at an infantile or adolescent developmental phase in the feelings, drives, imagination, and in mood-dominated ways of behavior is almost universally recognized today. A good part of the instinctual aberrations and perversions, of instinct shifting and compensatory addictions is clearly explained by such fixations.

Fear of the soul can also lead to a more or less conscious and obvious escape. Not only is there the escape from God, the manifold forms of which Max Picard has masterfully described, but one can also escape from the soul and take flight into areas which are then provided with comfortable furnishings. The area of escape can become a permanent residence which one only seldom attempts to break out of, so that its escape character slowly disappears and is repressed until, according to the law of enantiodromia, a psychic eruption necessarily takes place, inundating the fixation. Here we will merely allude to three escape areas which today seem to be the most favored.

Let us first look at the entire somatic area. The *escape into the sphere of the body* is a peculiar characteristic of our time. Organ neurosis, the point of departure of the psychology of the unconscious, shows a symptomatic that clings to a physical organ although its backgrounds are psychic: cardiac, intestinal, and vegetative neuroses, some forms of migraine, tics, partial paralyses, and so forth. Psychic disturbances are externalized and psychic conflicts are converted into physical symptoms so that the body, which has to be taken seriously, becomes the battlefield of repressed psychic crises. After all, people pay attention to physical ailments, while psychic difficulties are brushed aside as imagination, weakness of character, and malingering. Only when one has suffered from a true cardiac crisis can he expect the necessary care and consideration. Paradoxically, this overevaluation of the physical is typical even among the educated. The epidemic rise in the consumption of tonus-increasing drugs and tranquilizers also indicates a flight into the somatic realm. The phenomenon of addiction which is becoming more frequent in such cases is almost universally considered by psychiatry as a compensation phenomenon which is due to the lack of psychic ability to relate to others and to love (Szondi, v. Orelli). The body, however, becomes a refuge not only in serious crises but is often chosen prophylactically as an escape area. Some forms of physical culture, eurhythmics, and yoga may be mentioned here. Yet these tendencies primarily indicate a positive aspect: The body is besouled, and physical education and expression are also a psychic experience, though not always a forming and deepening of the psyche. The great value of these efforts should be acknowledged without resentment. However, we should see with equal objectivity that the somatic area has come to the dangerous stage of a mere hide-and-seek if it almost monopolizes the power of man and, because of its desirability, everywhere—in movies, radio, and television—pushes itself most matter-of-factly into the foreground.

Even more leveling and often almost soul-killing are the long-range effects of an *escape into the abstract and purely intellectual world.* Intellectual knowledge is valued as an important achievement; it is seen as the expression of the "higher man" and opens up immense spiritual areas in which man can organize himself. In the clean ozone of the intellect, superlogic is at first pleasant because of its unambiguity. There is no disquieting vagueness, no interference of insecure feelings, no factor of mood which perturbs or numbs, no speaker system which constantly stirs up emotions. Hence, the fascination of the intellect is frequently more dangerous than that of the body and can cause the soul to become mute, dry up, harden and congeal. All too often, especially in technologically oriented circles, we encounter poverty of soul, lack of feeling, one-sidedness, and crudity, leading far astray of the true picture of the human being, of full humanness. Here the world of masculine intellect looks askance at the feminine character of the soul, fearing that it may become effeminate and emasculated or at least be abducted into the labyrinth of uncontrollable feelings.

Perhaps we may admit that this masculine fear of the soul's femininity seems more justifiable today than before, since woman's soul-character is no longer quite so sure of itself; on the one hand, it yields to an unhealthy masculinization, and, on the other, it not infrequently takes flight into unconstrained hysteria. But precisely because of this, the soul's deep and true life is in greater peril and thus demands our utmost attention. For flight into the world of the intellect sooner or later leads to the irrationality of collective neuroses and collective psychoses: The law of enantiodromia will not be trifled with! Moreover: "Knowledge is power" and intensifies self-assertion. We will be the first to acknowledge that a mere education of intellect is tabooed today; everyone seeks also to cultivate the regions of the soul and thus awaken feelings for nature and art and social living. But all too often these efforts remain fruitless because they liberate psychic forces in an unbalanced and isolated way without bringing them into vital contact with the whole man, with his dynamic instinctual life and his intellectual fields of force. As a result, the awakened feelings become unstable and feeble and not infrequently degenerate into sentimentalities and their revolting consequences, or else they tend toward a free-floating moralism and rush the already overcultivated ego into a dangerous perfectionism. The lack of education of the soul becomes most strikingly evident in marriage conflicts. It is certainly no secret that many today enter marriage prematurely as is evidenced by the high divorce rate, especially among teen-agers. Instead of blowing up a storm of indignation, those responsible should first remind themselves that young people should not be released into adulthood merely on the basis of physical and intellectual maturity without also being on their way to psychic maturity. A primitiveness and lack of development of the life of sensitivity and feeling, of the entire world of imagination and mood have the most shattering effects on marital life and, therefore, by way of transference endow the subsequent generation with an increased deficit.

The most primitive but at the same time most frequent escape is the *flight into radical extroversion.* One leaps into "busyness," running from the social whirl and club craze into a superorganization of unimportant and highly superfluous arrangements. It is actually a plunge into the desolate flatland of exaggerated activity with its mightily arrayed apparatus of telephones, dictaphones, and intercoms, which echoes like the act of suicide of an impoverished and empty soul. This restless activism purposes to delude man as to his inner shallowness and psychic boredom. In the collectivity, in Heidegger's well-known "Man" (one), in Sartre's "situation," there is sought, and apparently also found, confirmation and protection. It is a torment for such people to be alone for half an hour and to feel unbusy and useless. Here the soul is already under the influence of narcotics, and it is now only a matter of becoming addicted to the display of some kind of ersatz soul in order to give oneself and others the sense of being irreplaceable. The cynicism of this attitude leads to the wildest paradoxical jumps. Then what is called work therapy proves to be only work hysteria that makes man run around in circles on the periphery of his being. The true inner center is replaced by the bottomless abyss of a psychic vacuum. For such people the mere reference to "soul" is suspect, and they defend themselves against their own conscience by calling every striving of the soul idleness, pathological self-reflection, or luxury.

This soul-anxiety—is it perhaps that the soul is so weak that it dreads confrontation with its own depth? Could this not be a legitimate reason for a flight into externalism? Should not the opposition to self-reflection and unhealthy self-analysis be taken seriously? Is it healthy to become so enmeshed in one's own inner world? But the counterquestion is even more justified: Are those who escape into busyness *really* those who could become the victims of a pathological cult of the soul? Simply posing this question is already to answer it in the negative in the majority of cases. One cannot escape from his

own soul without mutilating his life and also condemn-
ing himself to illness in the physical realm and to a
perfidious, stereotyped pseudo productivity in the intellectual. Just as the very short-lived attempts to escape
based on the fear of death can never be successful, neither, in the long run, can the different escape areas one
resorts to through fear of the depth of one's own soul
hide man from this depth. Time and again the soul,
from behind all curtains and stage settings, will sound
its voice, its alarming calls, its throbbing, restless complaints, or its cry of despair. And even the soulless man
reveals his betrayal through his rigid mask.

When, after our excursion into the regions of soul-
anxiety, we return to our point of departure and call to
mind the other basic forms of anxiety, the fear of death
and the fear of God, man stands before us as a fugitive.
The restlessness of the fugitive, so palpably present all
over the world, is actually nothing else but the articula-
tion of the common fate of man. The problem of the
fugitive hits each and every one. Is this fugitive an exile
or a deserter or both? How can he bear the fugitive's fate
without falling, in his uprootedness, into asocial, aggressive, criminal behavior or simply into that great apathy
in which man becomes indifferent to God, death, and
soul and begins to be allergic to all central questions of
existence? Should not all efforts to clarify this problem
be welcome whether they are undertaken by theology,
philosophy, or depth psychology?

No matter how arrogant it may sound, the fact is that
most patients must first be given the opportunity to reex-

perience their own soul and become more clearly and joyfully aware of its reality. Paradoxically, they live without soul in a desert of mere existence, concerned only with their vegetative needs, or in the cold region of "interests" and impersonal values. Even many a "religious" person has become alienated from his own soul. For him God is the ultimate solution to the problem of the right order of life scientifically surveyed by the technological intellect. The "practice of religion" (terrible expression!) is a means of someday reaching a distant, unknown goal. No wonder many, trying and trying again, grow tired and give up. Did not Carl Jung wisely say: "Even God cannot thrive in a soul-starved mankind"? Sometimes months of analytical effort must be expended in order to lead a person back to his soul and to the experience of this wider world. The soul with its moods, feelings, phantasies, with all its sensitivities and experiential nuances must be changed from a neglected, fallow field into a well-tended garden. Only after a gradual "in-spiration" can the difficult problems of life be seen in their true proportions and be solved. Then the central psychic power of a true love of life, of values, and of God can awaken. Such an awakening is like a new birth, giving life to what before was the deadly monotony of a trained puppet or a tired and weary human automaton performing acts devoid of meaning. Only then soul-anxiety has become in its deepest sense unnecessary.

CHAPTER III

Aspects of Development

Man can be understood only as a becoming, developing being. This basic dogma of depth psychology has nothing to do with the popular concept of development; rather, it puts to work the insights of modern philosophy, which include time and temporality as a fourth dimension of all living existence. Even though depth psychology is aware of the fact that man has an inherited psychosomatic constitution with very definite dispositions, and even though C. G. Jung's doctrine of the archetypes (the structure-given dispositions of the psyche which manifest themselves in primordial motives, images, and gestures) is certainly basic, depth psychology nevertheless emphasizes not so much the statics of this constitution and structure as its dynamics. All dispositions urge toward unfolding and development, and this urge is supported by the total psychic energy-potential. Man appears to be an electrically charged field of force. Whenever the effectiveness of the energies is hampered or interfered with, this field of force is in disorder and psychosomatic health is in peril. If man's development according to his dispositions is hindered or completely blocked, he experiences distortion and frustration of his nature in seemingly unmotivated depressions of inexplicable states of agitation. The urge to become and developmental dynamics cannot be ignored or falsified with impunity. The consequence of disturbed development or of misdevelopment is neurosis.

Psychotherapy, therefore, uses all possible means to reverse such developmental interferences and misdevelopments and to create and support more favorable conditions for a healthy growth of the psychic organism. Often, however, it is difficult to distinguish what is hereditary and structure-given and what is the outcome of development, of individual maturation. Thus, the more we succeed in finding a lawfulness in psychic development, in its range of variance and its favorable and unfavorable conditions, the more psychotherapy can become aware of its own possibilities and limitations and carry out its task.

Freud's developmental phases of libido, which have been repeatedly confirmed, already hoped to prove such lawfulness. But even the law of the "regulating function of opposites," as formulated by Jung, should not be misinterpreted as a mere balancing of the psyche into a static state of equilibrium (for instance, a static balance of conscious and unconscious). It is rather a matter of progression toward a relative psychic wholeness and completeness, of an eminently inner dynamic. Instincts, urges, and archetypes tending toward symbolic formation are in the service of this dynamic, which, thus, seems to be structure-given. It is an inner entelechy oriented toward the realization of psychic existence as a meaningful wholeness. Therefore psychotherapy, in so far as it is based on depth psychology, seeks to bring psychic energy to a relatively well-moving flow. Any damming up of this energy, which would entail the danger of a psychic thrombosis, and any uninhibited manifestations, which can lead to inundation of the psyche, should gradually come to a healthy, productive slope. By this we do not mean to interfere with temporary dammings, which can be of great importance, for example, to the creative artist and scientist, nor do we mean to advocate a flow of energy that is so even as to be monotonous; rather we wish to eliminate the extremely dangerous rapids.

But this powerful developmental dynamic is opposed by a peculiar tendency to fixate upon the phase that has been reached, to hold on and not let go at any expense. A stubborn, retentive force is clearly present. Moreover, the psychotherapist constantly meets the tendency to escape back to earlier phases and stages of life: to the romantic happiness of youth or even the dreamland of childhood. There is an almost insuperable inclination to escape into an unhealthy world of phantasy through the dream factory of novels and movies, or into oblivion through the euphoria of intoxication and drug addiction, or at least into the hectic ecstasy of modern forms of dance, and finally the complete regression into the womb of nature, which Freud probably had in mind when he felt the need of establishing the hypothesis of the death instinct. At first sight we face something incomprehen-

sible here. It is as if at times an inexplicable anxiety interferes with the impetus of development. Is it the fear of
losing what one has, what is familiar? Is it the fear of
losing the protection and security of the womb of the
family? Or is it the fear of the violent slope of one's own
energy? Fear of independence and responsibility? Or
does this fear go back to a last law of nature by which
man longs for the primordial state and strives to return
to it since he "is dust and must return to dust"? Is it the
"great tiredness" which Nietzsche seeks to avoid?

Life instinct and death instinct, progress and regress:
between these tendencies the drama of life is played.
They can lead to health or to neurotic illness. The urge
for an unrestrained, overhasty development and pseudo-
Faustian ecstasy is just as neuroticizing as is becoming rigid and hardened in a fixation, or the regression
symptoms which almost automatically accompany a
misdevelopment.

If we deliberately disregard the contents and values
which have to be realized through the dynamics of development, there is, besides Freud's aforementioned phases
of libido and Jung's law of the regulating function of the
opposites, hardly a psychic event, in my opinion, which
is so important to progression, fixation, and regression
as the constantly occurring event of identification. The
entire development of man is deeply affected and marked
by this event. An insight into the dimensions and meaning of identification, its formation and liberation can
open up essential aspects of development and make them
understandable.

IDENTIFICATION

Identification can be described as the psychic event by which a person more or less assimilates an object, be it another person, an idea, or a "value," to such an extent that he forms a psychic symbiosis with this other; he feels, thinks, acts and his entire existence palpitates in it. Whenever this function reaches its greatest intensity it arrives at a fusion of the subject with the object. Identification should, therefore, in no case be confused with a conscious or unconscious imitation. Rather, we deal here with the most inner consummation of the experience and suffering of a model, with the feeling of being one with an idea or a thing, as if it were "a part of me." There is a "participation mystique" with this other in which inner autonomy and independence seem to be annihilated and the person no longer experiences himself in his individuality and inexchangeable uniqueness. This profound assimilation and psychic union, which can indeed become a fusion, manifests itself even in the language of gestures, in the tone of one's voice, and in one's entire behavior. The identifying behavior then becomes a mechanism which functions more or less autonomously. The individual no longer takes notice of it and is hardly conscious of how much he lives through an *other*. He is completely surprised when someone brings it to his attention. Of course, this mystical participation allows many degrees of assimilation, of intensity, and above all of consciousness or unconsciousness.

Were this function of identification effective and significant only in childhood and adolescence, we would still have reason to stress its importance. But it retains its supreme influence during the whole of life and furthers or hinders all psychic and spiritual development. The statement that every relationship to an object is originally based on an identification can hardly be seen as an exaggeration by anyone who has looked into the matter closely. The ineradicable propensity to identify seems to be an indispensable dowry of our existence which, however, can also turn out to be a very dangerous poison. We are right in speaking of a very necessary, healthy, meaningful identification, but also of one that is dangerous because it is outmoded and oversized.

The identification of the infant with the mother is both a vital and psychic necessity. "During the phase of infancy we are, so to speak, a physical extension of the mother, or the mother is an extension of our ego."[1] Nevertheless, at this stage the cutting of the umbilical cord has already severed the even closer union (with the strong affective transference) of the embryo and the mother. But the psychic umbilical cord will remain intact for many years, and it will be a painful phase for both when it has to be cut. For this reason the severance is often not clean and clear. Psycho-spiritual development during early and later childhood certainly demands that the natural fusion of child and parents continue and that the functions of assimilation and of increasingly conscious imitation play their role. In this way, in con-

[1] Karl Stern, *The Third Revolution* (New York: Harcourt, Brace, 1954) 213.

tinuous flow, the manifold transferences of feelings and the mutual communication of phantasies, images, and thought processes take place.

This primordial relationship, the "primordial we" of mother and child, is expanded in the first year of life through the relationship with the father and also with brothers and sisters. Thus, new identifications make possible a loosening of the primordial identification. The minimal psychic tensions caused by this loosening already demand of the child the strength that he not allow the mechanisms to play simply a passive role but that he actively participate in their formation. The child experiences them as an expansion and widening of his horizon or, in the reverse case, as an insoluble conflict. In the first case identification becomes a necessary power of formation, an irreplaceable molding power *for the child*. In so far as the mechanism of identification accomplishes this, it is not only legitimate but indispensable. In the unfavorable situation, however, where an unsatisfactory identification with the parents takes place, serious developmental malformations will become noticeable. The boy who can never in any way identify with his father will only with great difficulty find the way to a natural becoming-a-man; he remains insecure, becomes sissified, perhaps a "mother's boy" with homoerotic traits. The girl who can only reject her mother will find it hard to experience herself as woman and will perhaps seek a solution in masculine behavior. When the identification with both parents is unsuccessful we can almost certainly expect poverty of feeling-life, indifference, psychic emptiness, and a psychic splitting in those who have more than average intellectual capacity.

The need for identification with the parents in early childhood must always be kept in mind and should not be deprecated because of the equally important factor that this identification with the parents must someday be thoroughly shaken loose, a process that generally should take place during the phase of opposition in adolescence. In the meantime, the world has become wider for the adolescent and new possibilities of identification have come to the fore: To some extent models are consciously sought, which one emulates and which one would like to put himself on a par with. Often it is initially a kind of hero worship which, furthered by legends, myths, and fairy tales, becomes a powerful impulse for psychic development. Later on there are living models—athletes, politicians, artists, scientists—who are emulated, through whom life is seen and challenged. Does the adolescent not identify with all the heroes he reads about? Is he not everything that he takes into his psyche and his spirit? (Scholasticism is right about the knowing subject: *Homo* [*cognoscens*] *est quodammodo omnia!*) Still later suprapersonal values and ideas can be placed at the center of psychic life, from which basis a new phase of development is scaled. This is the time of endless discussions about ideology, art, politics, religion. The consequent identifications lead to violent debates, passionate positions, fanatical statements and polemics. The "sense of mission" can awaken and together with it a maximum of identification. One, so to speak, embodies the ideal which is defended at any sacrifice.

But it can also be that the line of identification is continued with persons. Especially in adolescence enthusiastic friendships begin in which the friend is called the "alter ego" in order to indicate the indissolubility of the union and the absoluteness of the mutual exchange of the core of the person. Later on the "great love" breaks open, the "grande passion," in which identification is so perfect that the lovers say to each other "you are I—I am you" and feel drawn to union in flesh and blood. Indeed, did not Schiller, in his letter to Reinwald, call love a "voluptuous confusion of the natures" and ask the question: "The eternal inner tendency to immerse in the other creature or to devour it, to tear it, is this love?" The urge of identification reaches here the apex of its intensity and its strongly autonomous, mechanical unfolding. But is such an identifying love not one of the greatest educational powers? Does it not actually demand a constant keeping pace with the beloved and his further development? The entire developmental process thus manifests itself as an ever new process of identification. Therefore, how much it is consciously willed and how much it is an almost autonomous process is of no significance in regard to the fact itself.

The fact that the identification drive is a constant companion of man during his entire life and is always forming him anew is so striking it can hardly surprise us that this drive satisfies several needs. As we have already emphatically pointed out, the infancy identification is not only vitally necessary but is already at this phase critically important for psychic development, and, above all, for the emotional life. As development continues, the tendency toward identification becomes more important for the psychic structure and for the centering of the different psychic layers. The phase of "hero worship" and the imitation of models helps one find his true ego and discover the real center of his being. The variations of the objects of identification are tests for the possibilities and limitations of the ego. At the same time, identification serves as partial fulfillment of and abreaction for one's sense of self-worth: The child feels himself one with his hero and model, and so he experiences an intensification of self-confidence, an impulse toward increased effort. But the realization that he cannot carry out the identification with the "great" to the desired degree can gradually direct the urge of self-worth into healthier forms and into the consideration of his own authentic worth, leading toward the development of the ego-ideal. It is especially the gradual formation of the ego-ideal which makes possible sublimation of libidinal energies and control of exaggerated instinctual demands, consequently ameliorating and lessening deep-rooted anxieties. This identification with continually new models is of no less importance in its function of ego-protection against the often exaggerated demands of one's own family and environment, thus making it possible to sever unduly comforting fixations to long-outmoded objects of identification.

The multifaceted task of the single mechanism of identification helps us to see why it imperturbably continues to function even into old age. However, we will not sufficiently understand the essence and, in a certain respect, the significance of this event and will miss its deepest mystery if we do not see it as a continual process of transcendence. The glow and magic of every new identification lies in the fact that it is a crossing of new frontiers and a gaining of ground in the continent of the soul. The psychic development made possible by every new identification demands a transcending of relationships hitherto entertained and a loosening and widening of the present identification: The "die and become" is here a necessity, and this age-old wisdom receives precise confirmation through the depth psychological science of the soul.

But before we deal with the necessity of widening and loosening of every identification, we must discuss identification in its dangerous and damaging forms.

FALSE IDENTIFICATIONS

It is deeply alarming that one of our most necessary and productive functions can work against us. Depth psychology has amassed a wealth of factual material proving that a great number of psychic conflicts and neurotic illnesses originate in false identifications, and these facts are newly corroborated day by day. We face the frightening paradox that man's greatest enemies are the members of his own household (*"inimici hominis domestici eius,"* Matt. 10:36). A constant and faithful companion can turn into a deadly enemy; the pleasure of identification can become the burden of identification. When we consider the innumerable objects competing for our urge for identification, errors seem unavoidable. In fact, errors can begin so early that they are completely outside the pale of personal guilt. Who can blame the little girl who to please her father (or even her mother) acts like a boy, consistently developing her animus so that after twenty or thirty years she is fashioned in a masculine mold and all feminine feelings and psychic powers dry up and harden? This not infrequent false identification leads to the most serious neuroses and breakdowns, for in the long run nature will not allow herself to be thwarted and demands her structure-given right. Such a terrible misidentification makes others seem slight, even though they lead in completely wrong directions: for instance, the choice of an unsuitable marriage partner because of unresolved parental complexes, or the many mistakes made in choosing a career due to overidentification with artists, dancers, politicians, or religious models. Even the confidence man and pseudo inventor are in most cases products of misidentification.

A most common misidentification, in respect to the object, is seen in the great number of confused individuals who in the most matter-of-fact way identify themselves with their exterior appearance, their titles, offices, social class, or even their bank account and consequently neglect their actual being-person.[2] Even more common is the identification with the conscious half of one's nature.

[2] Cf. C. G. Jung's reasoning about "persona" in "The Relations Between the Ego and the Unconscious" in *Two Essays on Analytical Psychology (Collected Works*, Bollingen Series XX [New York: Pantheon] vol. 7, 1953).

Indeed, depth psychology's first great discovery was that it could show in what disastrously modest and unassuming ways man limits himself, narrows his existence, and misjudges himself in identifying with the image he has carried for years in his imagination and his conscious. Is it not nearly tragic that most people keep half of their life investments under lock and key in the cellars of their unconscious and make their everyday transactions with only small sums? Many seem to have no idea that they have thoughtlessly thrown whole bundles of psychic stocks into the wastebasket of their unconscious, thinking them worthless or perhaps even compelled by anxiety. They live with only half of their psychic potential. They look at the world with only one eye, just as they write, paint, and work with only one hand. It is a shame about the other hand and the other eye. From early childhood many have become accustomed (or, perhaps, later forced by their profession) to leave a large share of their psychical-spiritual values untouched and worthwhile functions unnoticed and undeveloped in the shadow of their unconscious. Only in rare moments do these undeveloped stocks risk an outbreak, and then, usually, they cannot find the "right word" but, blinded by the light, clumsily and awkwardly exhaust themselves in a wild rage and so are quickly pushed back into the darkness. Carl Jung was the first to draw attention to this shadow, and in his theory of types he has given very concrete suggestions for recognizing it. Analytic therapy purposes to show man how to integrate his "shadow" and thus become more capable of using his entire psychic potential. Here we can only heavily underline this most frequent misidentification. It leads to a psychic standstill, to decades of marking time, and, consequently, to an inexplicable unrest, to a vague feeling that something is not right, and finally to the formation of neurotic symptoms. Needless to say, these "fixations" can be observed in all classes of society, from the highest to the lowest.

Misidentification can be said to be an identification that, because of *excessive intensity*, reverses its constructive power and becomes destructive. Wherever the identification mechanism is active great quantities of energy are in play: The ideal becomes the "grande passion" and takes hold of the entire person, occupying his innermost depth and seeking exclusive possession of all his powers. Thus we can already see an outline of the great danger that the ideal may become a system of terror,[3] exercising tyrannical force and swelling into an overidentification. This overidentification so absorbs man that he has no energy left for other important problems of life; everything is sacrificed for it, and significant developmental components can no longer become active. To the degree that the ideal furthers development in a certain direction, to the same degree it obstructs development in other dimensions of existence. Despite the forced cultivation of a characteristic quality, something embryonic remains, a childishness alien to world and life, perhaps even infantilism. This overidentification can also carry with it an exaggerated sense of mission, coupled with pathologic fanaticism that may go as far as a quasi-identity with the

[3] Cf. Albert Görres, *The Methods and Experience of Psychoanalysis* (New York: Sheed & Ward, 1962).

identification-object. The paranoid, for instance, may identify with great figures of the past, Alexander the Great, Napoleon, or even with a numinous power, a divine person. The last stage of the urge of identification is characterized by the more or less complete loss of the real ego, and the person is finally plunged into an unreal world.

Finally, *permanent identification* must be seen as mis-identification in many cases. We have already mentioned the rigid attitude of many older people who become calcified with their obsolete ideas and hobbies. A classical case of a detrimental permanent identification is found when it goes back to the primordial identification, that is, the tie to the parents. In fact, even among older patients psychotherapy encounters at times very crass forms of the Oedipus and Electra situations, that is, of unresolved identifications with the parents. Miss L., very efficient in her profession and quite intelligent, at fifty-nine is still completely dependent on her eighty-five-year-old mother. She has no say concerning the arrangement of her own room, gives almost her entire income to her mother, and is scolded like a little child when she wants to go out in the evening.

The gradual severing of the primordial tie to mother and father that should take place during puberty is sometimes entirely avoided and at other times only partially achieved. In such cases the originally necessary and healthy identification turns into a misidentification and hinders psychic development. The parent-fixation can continue although the parents have been dead for years. Here the image of the parents still exercises a magic influence on the feeling life. All behavior is determined by this fixation and life-decisions are made or omitted in an inner dependence on them or in a lingering attitude of protest. An example of this is the thirty-five-year-old man who marries a woman ten years his senior and who cannot conceal his obvious symptoms of timid puberty in the face of her efficiency and practicality. He is a man well established in his profession who psychically has remained an appendix of his mother, to whom he has bound himself again in a new edition, and thus he is still "faithful" to his mother.

The most diverse experiences have illustrated over and over how a permanent identification turns into a mis-identification, and the inference that every permanent identification necessarily becomes misidentification and therefore inevitably leads to neurosis becomes an imperative when we realize that man, as a dynamic being, must progress developmentally. Seen in this way, the question of loosening and severing identifications becomes the problem of self-discovery, of becoming-person through the painful way of human development.[4]

THE LOOSENING OF IDENTIFICATION

Persons, ideas, and values that have once made deep inner connections belong to one's own life. They cannot

---

[4] It is obvious that here the value of true fidelity is in no way questioned, since this fidelity demands of persons that they know themselves responsible to their innermost core and to that of the other person, to the very core which requires a constant development and hence also the loosening of a too intense identification.

be simply eliminated or ignored. They have become a part of the ego, have been "insouled" and "inspirited." They can no longer be cut out of the psychic organism and surgically removed.[5] The identifications so necessary for psychic development cannot be simply undone. They have at one time penetrated into the deepest chambers of man's heart, have molded him, have been his happiness and his misery. Some of them will always be there with their positive and negative effects. But healthy development resolutely demands their loosening and their severing; the "die and become" is one of the most important laws of psychic health and development.

Presumably a need so stringently imposed can find sufficient help in a natural development process. Does not life approach man from the outside with such power and such an unceasing flux of impressions and demands that he cannot remain fixed? Is there not in the soul itself a restless blowing against the shelter of the present state, allowing no final comfort in one's achievements? In his depth psychological analysis Carl Jung encountered Heraclitus' age-old law of enantiodromia as a basic law of all psychic life, a law of utmost significance for psychic development in general since it constantly opposes the tendency toward identification with a countertendency. In serious cases this may result in a violent psychic power struggle, and sometimes the countertendency is vanquished, or it can cause the well-known phenomenon of ambivalence (for instance, love-hate). In

[5] Leucotomy effects a suspension of excessive emotionality rather than a change of psychic-spiritual contents.

any case it is a violent turmoil, shaking loose all identifications, bringing them into correct proportion in confrontation with their opposites and so lessening the influence of these identifications and even setting them at a distance.

The urge toward *opposition* is very often the first phase of the necessary loosening process. Why is it that in very close relationships we frequently find these mutual frictions, these small yet constant misunderstandings, and an unexplainable lack of consideration? Consciously, both parties seek not only to accept but to enhance their relationship. It seems as though in the unconscious a traitorous opposition is at work. The unconscious, which knows "more," which also wants to reveal the repressed and undeveloped capacities and functions, must skillfully or violently war against the ties of identification that cause a restriction of the entire person. The resulting situation is painful; increased sensitivity, unjustified reproaches, petty distrust, jealousy and envy play havoc with the hitherto good relationship. Yet this takes place only on a stage in the foreground which the unconscious is constantly calling to one's attention, while behind the scenes it is encouraging one to sever or at least to loosen an old, intense, and long-outmoded identification.

This opposition can take on massive and violent forms, for in some instances it is obviously in proportion to the intensity of the identification tie, at least in those cases where the unconscious life is instinctually healthy. Especially in adolescence this leads at times to very explosive scenes in the form of seemingly superfluous but often necessary power displays of an unfolding ego. But similar eruptions and aggressive attempts at liberation can take place in marriage and in friendships when one of the partners feels himself dominated by the other and hindered in his free development. Healthy nature rebels against fetters and against the bars of the playpen even though they are made of gold and inlaid with diamonds. This counterprocess against identification is always painfully felt, since it tears out a piece of one's own living heart. For the adolescent it very often results in feelings of loneliness: Is the entire environment not hostile? Is everything not strange and incomprehensible, empty and meaningless?[6] The countermovement against identification can also lead, in certain cases, to a complete negativism, a cold lack of contact, and come perilously close to a soul-killing emotional deep freeze. For although the ego can be devoured or suffocated by an oversize Thou, without such a Thou it may never come to life and experience itself profoundly and joyously as ego. Thus it appears that the true ego can stand up for itself only through the constant polarizing process of identification and the loosening of identification, of closeness and distance. What the psychotherapist most frequently encounters, however, is not a healthy opposition to identification but, rather, and inability to create such opposition.

Those who have not succeeded in breaking the tie of

[6] Hermann Hesse has masterfully represented this tormenting struggle of development in his novels *Demain*, *The Prodigy*, and *Magister Ludi*. His motto is always the same: "All I wanted was to try to live what wanted to come out of myself. Why was this so difficult?"

identification with the parent during adolescence will find it very difficult to be fully free. Parents represent "life forces whose influences even the adult can only conditionally evade" (Jung). Inwardly too many parents do not wish their son or daughter to be free. The child is always "their" child and their possession. Is the father who still calls his twenty-six-year-old son a little boy aware of what he is doing? Did Marcel Proust's mother realize what she did to her son when for more than thirty years she treated him as a little child? "*Pour Madame Proust, son fils Marcel avait toujours quatre ans . . .*" are the words of his nurse. In these and similar cases the dependency is at times unconsciously yet systematically, and often tyrannically, kept alive. Every slight illness or cold serves to tie the child even more closely to oneself; every failure in school or in training for a profession becomes proof that no one is so selfless as the parents. In the name of love or an almost blasphemous exegesis of the fourth commandment, the young person is cheated of his own life, and his process of maturation and his adulthood is thwarted. One keeps him away from everything, seeks to save him from all that life demands of him for a true and necessary confrontation.

"I am nobody," complained the twenty-nine-year-old daughter of a reputable family, who held a good position. "I don't take my person and my desires seriously. I never buy anything worthwhile, because it seems to me to be self-indulgence. What I want is not important. I think something has to be changed. I must be true to myself. . . ." There are parents who use all kinds of intrigues, some naïve, some quite base, in order to block any attempts of their no-longer adolescent sons and daughters to break away from them. On the other hand, this tie of identification to their "children" brings the parents themselves to a serious standstill in their own development. They remain nothing but "fathers" and "mothers," and their life would be empty, superfluous and meaningless if the "children" were no longer with them. In this way the fixation has a reciprocal effect that can hardly ever be resolved. Both parties are unsatisfied, for their unconscious disturbs them in the guise of a bad conscience (actually it is the "good" conscience at work), creating constant power struggles within their own four walls. But the opposition in these cases is usually as feeble as it is chronic: It exhausts itself in a cold war of attrition.

All these cases prove that opposition merely for the sake of opposition is a void that becomes more and more a fatally enveloping and narrowing vicious circle. To be meaningful and effective, opposition must be based on a new experience of, and insight into, value. The transcendence into this new value-world must take the place of the outgrown identification. This value-world can present itself as one's own life which now is experienced as truly worth living, even though from early childhood it may have been stressed as insignificant. It can also be seen as the relationship to a person with whom one seeks to establish a new community of life by his own free choice; or it can be a spiritual, artistic, social, or religious goal which shall become the content of life.

As early as 1924 Jung wrote: "A man cannot properly fulfill even the biological meaning of human existence if this and this only is held up to him as an ideal. Whatever the shortsighted and doctrinaire rationalist may say about the meaning of culture, the fact remains that there is a culture-creating spirit. This spirit is a living spirit and not a mere rationalizing intellect. Accordingly, it makes use of a religious symbolism superordinate to reason, and where this symbolism is lacking or has met with incomprehension, things can only go badly with us. Once we have lost the capacity to orient ourselves by religious truth, there is absolutely nothing which can deliver man from his original biological bondage to the family, as he will simply transfer his infantile principles, uncorrected, to the world at large, and will find there a father who, so far from guiding him, leads him to perdition. Important as it is for a man to be able to earn his daily bread and if possible to support a family, he will have achieved nothing that could give his life its full meaning. He will not even be able to bring his children up properly, and will thus have neglected to take care of the brood, which is an undoubted biological ideal. A spiritual goal that points beyond the purely natural man and his worldly existence is an absolute necessity for the health of the soul; it is the Archimedean point from which alone it is possible to lift the world off its hinges and to transform the natural state into a cultural one."[7]

Thus, in the name of psychic health, depth psychol-

[7] Jung, *The Development of Personality* (*Collected Works*, Bollingen Series XX, vol. 17, 1954) 85–86.

ogy demands a further development of man through relationship to a suprapersonal value-world. Of course it does not cherish illusions in this respect, as though it were easy to make progress in deepening one's spiritual needs and aspirations.[8] Rather, it is a matter of bringing into closer proximity that spiritual horizon which illuminates the penultimate and most essential positions of existence. Without a connection with this ultimate depth, man remains at the mercy of his identifications, which time and again will awaken escape tendencies in him, the yearning to regress into a dreamworld, a state without responsibility, a happy-unhappy oblivion and submersion.

The normal time for the new personal tie (for the child's is no longer sufficient) to the suprapersonal world of values is approximately at that point where the tie to the parents must be severed if it is not to remain permanently the strongest. True, the beginning of a career and the establishment of his own family might seem to completely occupy the young person at that time. Yet it should be clearly recognized that, even though these new tasks awaken and develop many personal powers, they never go beyond the family circle but are still only a problem of loosening old and creating new family ties and may soon lead to a psychic standstill. When this happens professional and family obligations often become burdensome and unsatisfying. At this point one is chal-

[8] Cf. Josef Rudin, *Der Erlebnisdrang* (1942), where the early forms and cultivation of the value-experience of the adolescent are considered at length.

lenged to take a new step in his development and aim at the higher value-world.

Identification and its loosening are in the service of psychic development. Without identification and its fixating effects there would be no present for us, no fruitful dwelling in a human soul-territory. Without the loosening of identification there would be no true future, no discovery and unfolding of the still unexplored psychic continent. Both, therefore, are a life-task that remains ever new.

In many of their dreams our patients are on the way: in a train, on a boat, in a car. Often they are on foot climbing a steep road. The way is a symbol indicating that psychic development must take place, that it is time to move ahead. There are many factors which can either further or hinder such development: external and internal experiences, confrontations with persons, intensive studies, the facing of great life-problems. What continues to be decisive in all these situations is how and to what degree man identifies with these experiences, values, persons, and ideas, and if, when, and to what extent he can again free himself from them. Behind both psychic tendencies, that toward identification and that toward its loosening, is the unspoken, alarming central question: Who am I? Since man is neither completely identical with the configurations and values of this world nor completely identical with himself, in the last analysis this question remains open and man is on the way, in knowledge or in premonition: "Everything evanescent is merely a parable."

CHAPTER IV

Depth Psychology and Freedom

Since its beginnings at the turn of the century, depth psychology has held a middle position between the physical-science-oriented, mechanistic elemental or association psychology and the philosophical psychology of Dilthey and his school. On the one hand, Freud through his investigations of organ neurosis rediscovered the influence of the soul on the body; he found the psyche in the senses. As a result both a purely sensistic psychology and an extreme reflexology (Pavlov) were kept within bounds from the very start. Moreover, the discovery of the unconscious realm of the soul with its impenetrable depth and collective primeval streams, its mythical primordial images and symbolic configurations (Jung), seemed to favor the renewal of a romantic concept of the soul. Thus depth psychology overcame the materialism of a "psychology without soul." On the other hand, depth psychology owed much to physical science and its methods. Therapeutic analysis attempted to discover the mechanisms of the psychic event and hoped to establish an entire energetics of the soul by a hypothetical application of the concept of energy. The principles of the constancy and equivalence of psychic energy have been demonstrated in the constructs of repression, compensation, substitution, sublimation, and psychic "arrangement." The principle of the natural slope of this psychic energy has been accentuated in "the regulating function of the opposites." At the same time it became evident that in establishing such laws of necessary and universally valid character the scientific claims of psychology were guaranteed.[1]

Because of this intermediate position, depth psychology has not infrequently given the impression of being irresolute and insecure in answering essential questions concerning the picture of man. Yet we should not forget that depth psychology has to depend upon the results of the actual practice of psychotherapy, which gives it ever new insights and constant corrections of premature systematic experiments.

Thus, today, depth psychology is challenged more and more frequently with the question of the *freedom of man* and its realization in the therapeutic conversation. Of course, we cannot predict what results may someday be empirically validated, but we should at least try to bring some light to this very complex problem. For, even though the particular facts referred to here are quite well known by the experts, the aspect of freedom under

[1] We may call to mind that the Church, too, is willing to acknowledge these mechanisms and determinisms of psychic life and their further investigation and consideration in human guidance and therapy. Cf. Pope Pius XII's address to the Congress of Psychotherapy and Clinical Psychology (April 7–13, 1953, Rome).

which we seek to interpret these facts is so little recognized that we can only feel our way through depth psychology's progress from an energetic-mechanical-final way of thinking to a thinking that also includes the category of freedom.

The concept of freedom is far from having an unambiguous and fully validated content. In saying this we are not so much referring to the metaphysical concept of freedom as inferred from an analysis of the spiritual components of man's nature but to a freedom that is, or seeks to be, psychically *experienced*, be it as a being freed from inner compulsive ideas and impulses or as the setting free of still unawakened, unfree, psychic powers; be it as a free decision in important situations, or as self-determination and self-development of the inner man. The experience of freedom has many layers and is therefore capable of progress—and yet it should be clear that such a progredient experience, by necessity, tends to reach the limits of an *idea* of freedom which is hardly realizable in the realm of experience but which, as a correlate of the spirit, must be postulated as a freedom made autochthonous by the fact of the spirit itself. Here, however, we deal with a freedom that can be experienced and gradually realized: the problem of depth psychology and the problem of the sick individual.

FREEDOM AS A
PROBLEM OF DEPTH PSYCHOLOGY

It is not the influence of a metaphysics or even of a dogmatic view of the image of man which has led depth psychology to the question of freedom. Neither does this question depend on existential dasein-analysis with its new approach to man in terms of decision and free life-project from a direction at first far remote from depth psychology. The stimulus for this question came rather from the *practice* of psychotherapy and depth-psychological theory. Certain facts cannot be ignored without furthering dangerous fixations within the person undergoing analysis. These are facts which postulate a certain realm of freedom within the psychic event. More exactly, this means that in the psychological process one touches upon a phenomenon of freedom and observes a psychic realm only partly controlled by mechanisms, since within this realm so-called free acts—for example, decisions and choices—also take place. This freedom-component can be discovered in many psychic behavior patterns, resonating in different degrees of intensity, at times almost imperceptibly. Two brief explanations will clarify this basic fact.

1.

Just as man's psychic event cannot be correctly understood when isolated from his body as such and its concrete gestalt, neither can it be sufficiently grasped when isolated from the specific *psychic* energy and the resulting capacity of decision. If we disregard parapsychological phenomena, the spirit-soul activity of man is closely connected with biologically and physiologically vital events, just as these latter are likewise almost constantly influenced by psychic energy.

In his book *The Structure and Dynamics of the Psyche* C. G. Jung writes: "Thus we arrive at the paradoxical conclusion that there is no content of consciousness which in another respect would not be unconscious. Perhaps there is also no unconscious psychic content which is not at the same time conscious." Therefore, we can say with good conscience that in many unconscious happenings there is a "piece" of consciousness.[2] Only its presence and activation make possible the intended process of enhancing the conscious, since something absolutely unconscious can never become conscious. But wherever the barest minimum of consciousness is present, there is also an initial capability of free decision, although this latter may seem almost beyond the limits of experience. But even a slight consciousness immediately creates a certain contrast, a small, inner distance of the conscious subject from the confronting object world. The complete identification and the participation mystique between subject and object is herewith loosened. The more brightly and clearly consciousness glows, the greater becomes the zone of distance and the finer the differentiation. From this distance-creating power of consciousness springs the possibility of a free decision, of a free choice, of willing or not willing to use one's energies, and of willing to use them in this or that way. The freedom of this decision is all the mightier, the less the subject is captivated, fascinated, or devoured by the object.

Take note, however: This same consciousness can so

[2] Jung expressly excludes the psychoid-unconscious since it comprises that which is unable to become conscious and is only a mimicry of the soul.

distance itself from the object, can so lose every contact and even capability of contact with a part or the whole of the object world that, splitting away, it becomes petrified in its subjectivity and is deprived of a free decision regarding objects, because it can no longer keep them in proper focus and they, too, slip away from its grasp.

It should now be very clear that the freedom of man allows many degrees, that its scope is wide and rich in nuances, but, furthermore, that it can never be absolute, for it depends on the material that it has to form and about which it should be concerned. Thus freedom is never only a freedom *of* but has always, since its beginning, been also a freedom *for*.

This constantly fluctuating level of consciousness and freedom (and unfreedom) of an act and of psychic events is probably one of the main reasons why every neurosis is one's personal property and why Jung wisely maintains that one should not treat case x according to Freud or Adler or Jung but always according to case x.

2.

This freedom is in some psychic acts a quite constitutive factor; it participates not only somehow marginally but *essentially* forms and stamps many even predominantly unconscious acts. For instance, closer observation shows that neurotic compensation is not completely compulsive. First Birnbaum and then, a few years ago, G. Kujath stressed the importance of a *self-chosen* system of compensation and control for the elimination of inner difficulties.[3]

In a like manner L. Szondi was compelled (1944) to give a new connotation to the "old-anankological" concept of destiny and to make a clear distinction between a forced and a chosen destiny, since only together do they form the personal destiny. He logically speaks of a new anankology in which freedom has its place.[4] We recall in this context that earlier Freud had emphasized the "overdetermination" of many psychic acts. But an overdetermination leads necessarily to the question of whether it is not the soul's power of free choice which allows certain determinants to become active while it makes others ineffective or keeps them in reserve.

It is above all Igor Caruso who in his *Existential Psychology* has clearly elaborated this fact. He strongly argues that "instinct *and* decision can be *simultaneous* factors of action and that it is not a question of *only* being compelled or *only* being free." He maintains, moreover, "it is essential that in the case of a free act one should not speak of it as decision *alongside* instinct. In his being-driven man moves within the forms of existence proper to *him*; and herewith man is already a being *sui generis* within the being-driven, that is, in instinct as such and not *alongside* the being-driven. And also in his decision (here again we mean *in* the decision itself and not alongside or before the decision) man is not a pure

[3] Cf. *Allg. Zeitschrift für Psychiatrie und ihre Grenzgebiete*, 1942, Bd. 120, 74–75.
[4] Cf. *Wissenschaft und Weltbild*, February, 1954, 15–19.

spirit, not a hundred per cent responsible." Therefore, for Caruso, too, the question is not so much whether man is determined or whether he is responsible, as *"how* he now expresses and makes effective his specific freedom *within* the psychophysical determinants in a uniform and solidly framed anthropological picture." Now we can also understand his clear statement: *"All* human achievements and failures offer two aspects: a causal, determined one *and* a meaningful, value-bound one." This establishes a demarcation of both a mere determinism and an existentialistic autonomism. Instinct and freedom often simultaneously *constitute* the psychic event in an almost inseparable interlacement.

These insights have made us realize that the aim of psychotherapy is not only the removal of interfering symptoms, thus allowing the free disposal of psychic energy, but also the development of a more conscious and free *human being.* A discussion of the aims of psychotherapy, however, carries us into a very disputed area.

Even very early the mere removal of interfering organic and psychic symptoms proved inadequate. In contrast to this, Carl Jung's way of individuation established a more comprehensive goal. This way of individuation, however, should by no means be considered a luxury therapy, since in most cases it is necessary if the patient is to attain an intrapsychic completeness and together with it a certain self-possession and freedom without which the mastery of internal and many external conflicts seems almost impossible. Thus, the widening of the realm of the soul means a widening of the realm of freedom.

Individuation can be equally necessary to enable man to find a *transcendent meaning* of life, without which many relationships toward the outside and toward the above would atrophy. Even a brilliant expert in the field of biological processes and reflexes and of the entire inner labyrinth could gradually lose sight of the outer realm of life with his fellowmen, of his profession, his marriage, of his connection with history and the imperishable world above and suffer the neurosis of an isolating insecurity and final meaninglessness. Only suprapersonal meaningfulness frees man from the narrowness of existence and from the fear of evanescence and confronts him with personal responsibility. Theoretically, this means that depth psychology must decide whether it is willing to go beyond the relieving of neurotic symptoms into Jung's way of individuation and the way of life-fulfillment through the transcendent question of meaning (Caruso) and thus solve its most characteristic "problem of the shadow." If depth psychology continues in the direction of anthropology and the person, this goal will necessarily have to be considered.

In the concrete case one will have to lead toward a freedom which the individual patient is able to achieve at that moment. Hence we admit there are many possible degrees of freedom. This also brings up the question of the "endless analysis" (better: the never completed analysis), for, as we know, man is not relatively healthy until he actually realizes the degree possible for him. Seen in this way we can consider freedom as a "progressive freeing" of the patient, whereby the sequence of the three above-mentioned phases may in practice be quite varied.

Thus it seems evident that depth psychology is also in the "service of freedom"; in fact, it is, as Caruso poignantly put it, a "maieutic of freedom."

FREEDOM, A PROBLEM OF THE NEUROTIC

If we have succeeded in proving that for the neurotic the experience of freedom in thinking and feeling and above all in his unconscious psychic processes occupies a central position, then we will have arrived at important conclusions for the psychotherapeutic conversation. Therefore, first we shall try to examine the more or less manifest *attitude* of the patient toward his freedom in order to further consider the deeper *backgrounds* of this attitude.

The Attitude of the Neurotic Toward Freedom

Most human behavior is ambivalent, since only in the rarest cases does the human way of being reach that final and unambiguous completeness and absoluteness that is no longer a combination of absolute and relative aspects.[5] It is characteristic of the neurotic's situation that he unconsciously does not admit this ambivalence but wants to be always "absolute." Thus, in accordance with well-known laws of energy, the neurotic becomes in an especially crass way a victim of this ambivalence. Two contradictory series of sensations, feelings, imaginations,

[5] Caruso wrote strikingly about this ambivalence in "Die Wiener personalistische Tiefenpsychologie als symbolische Teilerkenntnis der menschlichen Person" (Beiheft 1 der Sitzungsberichte, 1953–54).

and trains of thought clash in him and radically provoke each other, making him inwardly restless and almost incapable of clear decisions and straightforward acting. This ambivalence reveals itself in a strongly conflicting attitude toward freedom. Therefore, one is inclined to speak of attitudes rather than of a single, typically characteristic attitude.

Despite this fact, part of the therapist's difficult task is to discover the preponderance of one attitude to which the patient only afterwards—even though very soon— develops the opposite attitude as a psychic counterpoint. Even in cases where this assumption does not hold true since the ambivalence appears to be primary, it seems worthwhile for the sake of method to elaborate as much as possible this specific attitude, for to its intensity corresponds the intensity of the counterattitude.

In the neurotic person we can clearly distinguish four different attitudes toward his freedom, two belonging to the affective-emotional layer and two more to the intellectual layer, seeking as *raisonnement* to justify the affective behavior and, hence, to overlay and reinforce it. It seems to us, however, that behind these four attitudes there is always a latent basic attitude which time and again comes to the fore: the longing for inner freedom.

1.

A great many neurotics have *fear* of their own freedom and its responsibility. This fear automatically manifests itself as a flight from freedom. The individual unconsciously maneuvers himself into situations in which, without personal freedom and responsibility, he is at the mercy of events. In this instance the various mechanisms of repression function as excellent escape mechanisms. But can this escape ever be a complete success? Does not the word *repression* already point to a repressing power? Before the mechanism of repression began its silent and skillful unconscious functioning, was there not at least one short moment when the person, even in a dim flash, decided in favor of the repression? Where he determined himself with a small grain of freedom? We have already seen that compensation does not take place altogether compulsively. In some instances an "arrangement" is set up, maybe an escape into illness. Can this happen without some kind of an original silent agreement of the power of personal decision? Should one not ask who is doing the arranging? Only the unconscious? Does not consciousness have at least its little finger in the pie? Or: when the "resistance" becomes transparent to the therapist in seemingly insignificant signs, does he not at the same time observe something going on behind the scenes of consciousness, but behind scenes that are by no means hermetically sealed? Why does resistance increase at the very moment when the compulsion begins to reside?[6]

[6] H. Müller-Eckhard has an interesting essay concerning this in *Psyche* (May, 1954, 149): "Among many patients suffering from compulsive manifestations there is an obvious *pleasure* in getting rid of freedom. Compulsion, when defined in the sense of Schopenhauer's negations, is nothing but the freedom from freedom. . . . In the compulsive symptom a new magic freedom is created which, as we will later see, is only a seeming freedom but nevertheless is experienced as freedom and in turn re-creates anxiety."

The mere possibility of catching others or oneself in repression, in arrangement and resistance, the mere fact that one is able gradually to recognize and control these mechanisms, does this not mean that at the periphery of these mechanisms there is a power waiting and wanting to have more to say in this matter? Does it not mean that there are not too many psychic mechanisms which function completely isolated from conscious psychic powers and their freedom?

One cannot but think that in many repressions the first thing repressed is the grain of freedom. But this means fear of and flight from freedom. In the collective neurosis this fear and flight become especially conspicuous, since there is such a need for the anxiety-dispelling and easily available scapegoats: Jews, Negroes or such cultural phenomena as technology, sports, fashions, and Communism. Dostoevski's Grand Inquisitor stated very bluntly that the masses do not endure their own freedom, but always look for one whom they can burden with it as soon as possible. They wish (and this "wishing" is the miserable remnant of their "freedom") to remain children without responsibility, still projecting their collective idols. When failure occurs, the guilty one must be quickly found. Of course, even the Grand Inquisitor has his scapegoat: the masses themselves and their fear of responsibility, for which he "sacrifices himself." He, too, now has a psychic alibi which he so often calls upon! He, too, fears and flees the freedom that he pretended to accept.

2.

In clear opposition to our first-mentioned attitude, we very often meet the *fear of the loss* of freedom. One is constantly concerned about losing his freedom and shrinks from conscious and responsible commitment. Very rarely, in actuality, is this the fear of losing a truly strong and service-minded freedom but rather an almost pathological fear of the loss of a puny, negative freedom that is held on to for its own sake in the form of a nearly complete lack of commitment. Freedom here means lack of commitment, lack of contact, fear of responsibility. In its immediate retinue we generally find an incapability of decision. These individuals want and they don't want; they are torn between their assumed freedom and provisionary commitments. Important life-decisions (marriage or choice of a profession) are postponed for years and the moment of decision causes such violent fluctuations that finally everything returns to the same old state—undecided and unresolved. These people always want the very thing they do not have, what is almost unattainable—and as soon as they can attain it, it ceases to be interesting to them and reveals its dark sides. The disturbing thing is that the passionate striving of the individual seems quite authentic and sincere. For instance, he forces himself to agree to a partnership which he immediately rejects as soon as the other agrees to it. In such a case the problem of freedom is quite evident and extremely acute, but, ironically, an inner psychic lawfulness, especially in this chronic fear of one's own freedom, in this lack of commitment and incapability of decision, causes also a loss of

external freedom. Then, almost by necessity, various circumstances and momentary constellations become the
decision makers and thus rob the person even of his
feeble remnant of freedom, creating a fatal vicious
circle of greater fears.

In addition to these two affective attitudes toward
one's own freedom are two other attitudes of a more
intellectual character. They usually appear as overlays
on or embedments in the more affective attitudes. Yet
among intellectual individuals they can sometimes even
be prevalent. (The conception of neurosis as an exclusively affective disturbance seems to us too one-sided.)

3.

In the first attitude of intellectual character we meet the
underestimation of one's own freedom. The patients see
only the alarming, conspicuous symptoms: their heart
irregularities and stomach cramps; they experience depressions or inferiority complexes, chronic fatigue or states
of irritation, discover a lack of concentration or even sexual impotence, complain about failures in professional
life, in love, about a lack of contact—and on and on.
They remain attracted to these symptoms as though spell-
bound. At best, they look for causes in their own physical deficiencies but more often in the behavior of the
outside world. With much logical keenness they choose
a "scapegoat" from their environment. The possibility
that a grain of their own freedom could be present in
their symptoms is almost unthinkable to them, for they

are too much taken up with their need of sympathy. It is obvious that fear of and flight from freedom easily hook into this attitude. This coupling causes the affective violence that accompanies all intellectual acuity in search of scapegoats and constantly stimulates all logical *raisonnement*, so that the question arises whether feeling is the servant of the intellect or the intellect the torch-bearer of feeling.

4.

This intellectualistically inhibited attitude becomes even more evident in the case of *overestimation* of one's freedom. For instance, patients may display an excessively guilty conscience which incessantly probes the hiding places of the soul in search of some fugitive particle of guilt. They blame themselves not only for their own failure but also for that of their surroundings and even of an entire community. They never get rid of their doubts, worries, and anxieties. Of course, in these cases, too, the coupling of their fear of freedom with the fear of the loss of freedom reaches an unbearable pitch. Self-gratification and self-hate go hand in hand. Such persons torture themselves in a sadistic masochism and develop a pathological need of assuming the role of the scapegoat. Thriving in this psychic climate are the tendencies of self-destruction, which at times can take on terrible forms.[7]

We will not deny that often enough in these cases

[7] Cf. S. Streicher, *Die Tragödie einer Gottsucherin, Margaretha von Wildensbuch* (Einsiedeln, 1945).

there may be a justifiable sense of guilt which one does not want to admit to himself. In our context it is of primary importance that these patients are able to experience the problem of freedom as the very central one.

5.

The more effective any one of these four attitudes toward freedom is, or the closer the coupling of several of them, the more disquietingly arises the *longing* for a true freedom. Most persons undergoing analysis suffer from their inner lack of freedom. Presentiently they recognize their compulsive state, their being driven, their dependence; they sense that time and again they are the prey of exterior events and even more frequently fall victim to their own inner imaginations and impulses. Finally they experience their lack of freedom as a restriction of their being-person. "I am nobody," they may complain, although they may hold important jobs. But inhibitions, inferiority feelings, guilt complexes undermine their self-confidence, make a healthy, secure self-respect impossible, and create a very unstable, dangerous condition. Their longing for freedom grows in proportion to the loss of this freedom through compulsive mechanisms. This longing can be a final rebellion of their nature, which knows itself called to a freer attitude. The longing for freedom manifests itself as innermost basic attitude even in an individual driven by compulsive mechanisms. Therefore, neurosis is also a crisis of freedom.

The Backgrounds of This Attitude

We have deliberately chosen the expression *background* in order to avoid the concept *cause* and also to replace a merely causal thinking with a more organic reflection. At the same time it must be emphasized that we have no intention of limiting this background to a single one. We do not wish to yield to the quite understandable human tendency toward reductive thinking, except when this kind of thinking seeks admission with valid credentials.

Disregarding certain organic-physiological defects which postulate a spiritual debility and so also a more or less complete lack of a true power of freedom, we can distinguish two kinds of backgrounds: the psychic and the metapsychic.

1.

Childhood traumas play the most important role in the psychic background. Freud is certainly to be taken seriously when he places the responsibility for the erroneous attitudes of children in the laps of parents, teachers, and clergy. It is a matter of fact that fixations upon an infantile phase, regressions to earlier developmental phases, replacement of the unattainable goals of the sexual and assertive urges with more easily achievable goals, and finally identifications with lofty ideals or persons (as perfectionism and "angelism") are a constriction and often a fettering of the sphere of individual freedom (even though a kind of self-defense mechanism against the adult is functioning in the formation of these phenomena). We find childhood traumas above all in the attitude of a pathological fear of the loss of freedom, in the chronic inability to commit oneself through decisions. Under the pressure of education, self-confidence could not healthily develop, the ego could not adequately be constituted, and the capacity for a secure personal decision could not gradually be formed. Thus there remains only an understandable fear of the loss of the freedom of one's own ego—and the instinctual, egotistical "id," which succumbs to the expediencies of the moment. Many exaggerated guilt complexes and, consequently, overestimations of freedom do not originate autochthonously in the experience of a personal conscience but are heterogeneously formed through an overstrict and conscience-deforming education, as proved repeatedly by depth analysis. The tragedy of what is called the "old school" is that, while it certainly desired the freedom of man, it too often tried to achieve this by way of unfreedom.

Carl Jung has convincingly demonstrated that another aspect of the psychic background is the *lack of development* of certain psychic functions and psychic images. The problem of the "shadow"[8] raises the question of a psychic completeness that seems to warrant a greater inner realm of freedom and so can at least awaken the attitude of longing for such freedom. In a similar way the

[8] Regarding the problem of shadow, cf. pp. 45–46.

striving for an elastic, well-fitting "persona"[9] is a striving for a greater freedom in external adjustment to the environment—and the integration of the projections of anima and animus[10] can free one from very serious compulsive states. Finally the integration of those symbols considered to be the concrete forms of universal human archetypes can in some cases be in the service of a deeper understanding of life and so also in the service of a greater inner freedom. Carl Jung's way of individuation overcomes a superficial underestimation of the individual's potential and of human freedom.

The *collective situation*, too, is part of the psychic background. Today's organized control of the state, of professions, of marriage, and of economics can often no longer shelter or even support man. But this does not mean that the realm of freedom has therefore broadened; on the contrary, the less stable individual in particular is either swept away by the unleashed streams of life or else feels himself gripped and threatened by political, economic, and technical forces with which he can in no way cope. These are anonymous, collective coercive

[9] The concept of "persona" as introduced by Jung should not be confused with the concept of person; rather, it is to be understood in the opposite direction. *Person* refers to the innermost center and metaphysical core of man, while *persona* indicates the manner and way in which an individual appears to his environment and—more or less consciously —represents himself to it.

[10] Anima-images are very deep-lying psychic images of the woman which the man bears within himself. Animus-images are corresponding images of the man which the woman has deep in her unconscious soul-ground. Since everything unconscious is projected, these psychic images of the opposite sex are also projected time and again to the outside, above all in the encounter with the opposite sex.

powers which no personal decision can adequately face. Under the guise of many advantages they take the decision out of man's hands and by this alone already weaken his capacity for personal decision. The collective situation must be considered co-responsible to a great extent for the attitude of *underestimation of freedom* and also for the pathological fear of *loss of freedom*.

2.

The psychic background, understood in this sense, can in many respects explain the crises of human attitudes toward freedom. Nevertheless, there are still open questions. A better understanding of the two attitudes of overestimation of freedom and of the fear of loss of freedom seems especially needed. In both attitudes the consciousness of freedom is relatively strong, be it as an exaggerated guilt feeling that is difficult to calm, or as an inability to make decisions that has its paralyzing effect on one's entire life and necessarily makes one aware of the problem of freedom as such. Here we touch almost directly upon the power of freedom, which represents an *autonomous* capability beyond the psychic happening and as such seeks to make its appearance. This means that the aforementioned psychic backgrounds can no longer adequately clarify these attitudes and a *metapsychic background* opens up to demand our attention. Freud himself once wrote: "Health cannot be described other than metapsychologically" (*Die endliche und die unendliche Analyse*).

In his universalistic depth psychology Igor Caruso is anthropologically correct in combining the intrapsychic mechanisms with the freedom factor and giving the latter its actual basis: the *category of transcendent meaning and value.* Only in respect to this category is man permitted to yield in full freedom to his absolutizing tendency without having to suffer guilt feelings and, through their repression, to be subjected to permanent neurotic conflict. But every false absolutizing of immanent goals must sooner or later—as "life-heresy," so to speak—lead to neurosis and to a crisis of freedom. Thus it takes on, in addition to the psychic, a moral, perhaps even religious, background.

It may be worthwhile in this context to refer to those "life-heretical" images of man which can be back of the *false attitudes* toward freedom and have a codetermining influence on the pathological process. Is it devious to say that behind the *underestimation* of freedom and its all too self-evident mechanisms of repression there is a materialistically interpreted image of man causing the free spiritual traits gradually to vanish, so that more and more man is considered as a determined being? On the other hand, do we not find a last hidden background of *overestimation* in the spiritualistically distorted image formed by one who seeks to ignore all intrapsychic determinants, in order to live—saintly or guilt-ridden—as a pure spirit, an angel? Finally, there is the question of whether the pathological fear of *loss of freedom,* with its paralyzed power of decision and its terrible confusion, can be adequately understood with the help of the psychic background. An overstrict education which never gave the child his rights, constantly oppressed him, and so destroyed a healthy self-confidence does not make it inevitable that in later years this person cannot find a better self-stand through a meaningful image of man related to ultimate values. Individuals who no longer have a solid, self-evident ego and only hold a few pieces of it in their hands may have formed their image of man out of a last insecurity and a meaningless despair: a practically *nihilistic* image of man. Of course, we should not overlook the fact that the inability to believe and confide in meaningfulness is in turn strongly conditioned by the experiences of these individuals.

After our discussion of freedom and neurosis there can be scarcely any doubt that freedom is a central problem of the neurotic. Neurosis is also a crisis of the freedom of man, and this means that beside, within, and behind the psychic influences are also metapsychic claims which demand attention, for freedom in its full meaning and in its actual, final understanding is a correlate of the spirit that is part of the nature of man.

THE REALIZATION OF FREEDOM
IN PSYCHOTHERAPEUTIC CONVERSATION

Let us not go astray in our conclusions from these reflections. It is not a matter of simply abandoning hitherto accepted principles and methods of the therapeutic conversation and replacing them with freedom as the center. Although the freedom component must frequently be recognized as a constitutive factor in neurotic behavior, in no way does this invalidate a careful analysis of the mechanisms. Especially in the case of those neurotics who are forever worried about their freedom, these mechanisms play an extremely significant role and need to be made conscious in order to create room for a true freedom. As for some other types of neurotics, one should be aware that their realm of personal freedom hardly admits of greater expansion, and, therefore, treatment should not aim too high in this regard. Nevertheless, freedom should be taken into consideration more than it has been up to now. Only this gives the patient the sense of authentic being-man, of a self-stand, which in the neurotic is generally seriously injured, bent, already half destroyed, and, possibly, at the same time exaggerated— but which urgently seeks a true formation.

It should also be immediately obvious that this is not a matter of speaking repeatedly about inner freedom or of even demanding it of the patient by constantly making him aware of it. Freedom must find its expression indirectly and naturally and therefore must influence the attitude and behavior of the analyst as well as the analysand. Thus we must take into account the attitudes and behavior of both patient and therapist.

The Attitude of the Patient

The very fact that the patient has decided, after careful consideration, to undergo treatment with the therapist lets neurosis be seen also as a problem of decision that engages a certain freedom of the patient. After all, he could avoid the treatment as time-consuming, expensive, and not necessarily leading to success. He could put up with his symptoms, for they are sometimes advantageous. The decision for therapy must be understood not only from the aspect of an external need but also as an act of freedom and must be evaluated according to its intensity. Various kinds of resistance which come up during the treatment can create doubt about the decision and require that it be freely renewed. Since these decisions are often very difficult, one cannot underestimate their positive significance for successful treatment. At the same time, the free decision gives a hint as to the background of freedom within the neurosis.

The treatment itself demands from the patient a constant inner "Yes" to the freeing process. Theoretically, this process takes place in four phases, although in actuality they may be fused. In the first phase it is necessary to create an inner distance to the interfering psychic events. Making these events conscious means to take them out of the identifying sphere of the subject and allow the ego to confront them as objects. They are externalized, objectivized, and thus the neurotic can give them distance. Only when the psychic contents with which one was formerly identified are placed at a distance from the ego can they be adequately distinguished from the ego and from each other. Every therapist who has had experience in dealing with complexes resulting from difficulties with parents knows how difficult this process of distancing and objectivizing can be. The separation and distancing of these contents from the ego enables the patient, in the second phase, to make clearer distinctions. He can now separate in a more precise way the positive from the negative and recognize the meaning they have within themselves as well as their meaning for his own life. His sense of value gains strength and security.[11] The neurotic wants everything at once, he inadequately distinguishes and does not accept values as such but unconsciously views them merely as an enhancement of his own importance or as material to be experienced, usually in a purely quantitative sense. Only after he has learned to distinguish is the third phase possible, in the form of a freer position in a freer decision. The fourth phase consists of self-control and the practice of freedom, in the sense that we have already developed. This, of course, is most difficult. Except for extreme cases it will generally be best not to separate the patient from his present life-situation, whether it involves problems with his family or in professional life; otherwise he will be deprived of necessary training. In the everyday situation his improvement will be very gradual. Time and again he will experience failure, but he will tend more and more to attribute it to himself rather than to his environment. Meeting these situations he learns patience and thus gains freedom through his own reeducation. In establishing a personal protocol he learns how to understand his

[11] We may point out here that this experience of distance and distinction from one's own ego can be called an empirical experience of one's spirit-ness. By distancing, the spiritual being experiences himself in his self-stand with a certain independence and irreducibility of a higher level of being. Cf. Hans Kunz, "Das Problem des Geistes in der Tiefenpsychologie" in *Psyche*, 1951, no. 5, 245–46.

freedom and to preserve it, even in the presence of his therapist.

In all of these four phases, however, the goal of freedom is unmistakable, and the patient experiences an opening up of the gates to greater realms of freedom as he breathes in fresh and healthy air—but he must be ready to take all four steps, each requiring a new decision. There is no need to say the word *freedom*; it is experienced interiorly and exteriorly and, above all, made real through the behavior of the patient himself, who must bear the brunt of the burden. The freeing process depends entirely on this new attitude toward freedom.

The Attitude of the Therapist

Obviously, the therapist can be no more than the midwife of his patient's freedom. Freedom can in no case be forced upon an individual, it can only be summoned and supported. Nevertheless, it depends essentially on the attitude and behavior of the therapist whether this freedom is to be a living creature or a still birth. Needless to say, only a therapist who himself possesses a high degree of freedom can lead another toward freedom. But does anyone ever possess freedom? Inasmuch as freedom is decision and self-determination, must it not be attained always anew, and sometimes in more difficult circumstances than others? Yet perhaps this very freedom, in the sense of psychological liberation, is not so much the achievement of an ever new existential decision but, rather, a continuous psychic attitude which can also be cultivated. This attitude should be consciously sustained by the therapist himself, lest through the transference of his own unfree attitude he hurt his patient rather than help him.

Freud's interpretation of the therapist's attitude toward freedom was that it be a kind of *tabula rasa* which is not a robotlike, rigidly inhuman attitude but one that is fully empathetic to the conflict situation of the patient yet consciously restraining from three things: First, it must restrict itself from any kind of moral judgment, be it incriminating or excusing, since this would make many patients immediately closemouthed, even though it might be very welcome to some. However, it is certainly always out of place with the compulsive patient. Secondly, it is absolutely imperative that the therapist avoid yielding to affect in the form of sympathy, compassion, or his own instinctual tendencies, for the patient's emotional attitude is to be gradually replaced with a calm and realistic view. A false pity, wishing to relieve the torment too quickly, can defeat the whole treatment. Here the old saying is all too true: one must let the patient stew in his own juice. Thirdly and finally, there must be freedom from the *furor sanandi*. The analyst who seeks quick results and is entirely set on ridding his patient of his symptoms, without keeping in sight the whole person in his development and in his freedom, is in danger of becoming a skilled craftsman in the power of suggestion, who brings about many false starts which are only temporarily helpful and do not lead the individual to authenticity and adulthood.

But now let us think more positively: Should the analyst have the freedom of the patient consciously in mind or should he rather direct his entire attention to the unconscious mechanisms and their connecting threads? If we are correct concerning the complex character of the psychic event, that it is at the same time determined and free, it should be possible for the analyst to pay attention to both components. This, of course, demands of him an attitude that is all the more sensible and alert, which does not become tense but remains relaxed and open toward the total behavior. Freud speaks of a "hovering attention" instead of a tight attention.

In addition to the permanent attitude of the therapist, we must take a thorough look at him in action. In the practice of therapy three temptations must be overcome: The will should never be directly appealed to, neither with strict nor even with mild demands. Once the patient has gone through the effort of bringing the background of his symptoms to consciousness, he sees his task clearly enough without having to be ordered, and until the basic conflict has become conscious every appeal to the will can only lead to a stronger repression of the actual source of the neurosis, thus causing an intensification of the neurosis with its old or possibly new symptoms. Equally detrimental is every premature explanation of the disease. Such an interpretation generally hinders both the therapist and the patient from pushing the analysis far enough and fully uncovering the incriminating material, so necessary for a true liberation. Therefore, in serious cases a "brief analysis" seems impossible. It is also impossible to lead a patient toward freedom if one relieves him of his decision by telling him what is to be done in specific situations. Even though this may be necessary in very rare cases, one should strive to leave the decision more and more up to the patient. One educates toward freedom by allowing the exercise of freedom.

Besides these general and rather negative rules it will always be difficult to establish rigid norms of behavior for the therapist. Some insist that the therapist must by all means maintain the role of a passive, detached spectator, while others (Rank, Ferenczi, Maeder) insist on more activity and direct guidance. Some agree with Freud that successful analysis demands the therapist's noninvolvement; others consider a warm, cordial, personally engaged atmosphere the most conducive to success. In this latter view one speaks of curing by making conscious, curing through confrontation, through personal action put to work. Sometimes these differing opinions take on the form of a radical either-or, as though there were only one *conditio sine qua non* of successful treatment. Other therapists, however, are more flexible and hold an as-well-as position, for in the course of the great analysis one kind of behavior may at times be adequate and at other times the opposite seems unavoidable. What is really at bottom is the delicate problem of transference, which therefore so often becomes the center of discussion.

Without entering into the details of this problem here, these seemingly incompatible opinions can be explained and justified only by seeing psychotherapeutic treatment as a freeing process that necessarily varies in each individual case.

A differential diagnosis of the crisis of freedom, especially of its individual backgrounds in the individual patient, must also influence the behavior of the therapist. In those cases in which the specific psychic backgrounds are evidently the main cause of the crisis, whether as childhood traumas or as lack of psychic development, the therapist as an incorruptible witness will, in the sense of the classical theory, have to accompany the dialectical process between the conscious and unconscious. Here, any yielding, any too persuasive attitude leads to dangerous half-measures. But it is entirely otherwise in cases where a collective situation has paralyzed or even strangled the psychic power of decision through a constriction of the realm of freedom and also in cases where the therapist finds himself in almost direct confrontation with the patient's autochthonous power of freedom, since the metapsychic category of meaning and value is directly visible as a psychic-spiritual pivotal point. In such therapeutic situations would not the dialogue of a true, personal encounter between physician and patient be in place? It is important that the patient find a sphere in which he can be completely himself, where he is allowed to express himself freely and in mutual, cordial openness and understanding. The "metapsychic core" of the patient must then meet the personal center point of the physician. Indeed, the more exact differentiation of the crisis of freedom and its specific backgrounds, therefore, contributes to the clarification of the transference problem.

In order for the therapist to maintain a positive attitude toward the realization of freedom within the patient, it again seems very important to us that the self-healing tendencies be carefully noticed, awakened, and furthered. Credit must be given to Alphonse Maeder for having always emphasized this viewpoint. The recognition of false attitudes, defense mechanisms, and blockings is generally more natural for the keen eye of the therapist than an equally precise observation of the sthenic powers, of healthy and positive ways of reaction. Yet, obviously nowhere are the powers of liberation more powerful than where the self-healing tendencies are already evident. Is this will to health and urge to be healed sufficiently probed and sought for in its concrete forms behind the masks of neurotic symptoms? Here, too, an insight into those sometimes longed-for, or sometimes feared, forms of freedom within the patient will prove very valuable. Since the self-healing tendency is basically oriented toward the establishment of the wholeness of the organism, the hidden but latently effective image of man is also significant. It is either in a harmonic tension or in a neuroticizing countertension to that other image of man which is perhaps consciously striven for. Thus, once again the crisis of freedom can offer a clue to the corresponding metapsychic background. In the specific tension between the primordial image and the de facto image of man which is aspired to we will find the concrete form of self-healing tendencies. Freedom plays an important role in this tension. The therapist's task is to find out whether this tension has the right intensity in a positive sense or whether it proves to be too weak or too strong because of serious neurotic symptoms. The setting up of a healthy tension relationship thus becomes a realization of freedom.

In the course of our explanations, freedom has more and more insistently become a key concept of the psychic event. Precisely because this freedom represents itself in ever new forms in the various stages of its realization process, it shows itself as the original power belonging to the whole of human life and seeking to participate in life's inner formation. It strives again and again to go beyond the state achieved, and so has a transcendent character. It seems as though in the subjective performance of its realization an objective state of our being-man is to be actualized: the human person.

CHAPTER V

Personal Life

REVIVAL OF THE PERSON

Today it seems almost inconceivable that for decades the concept of man as a person was abandoned in scientific circles. Man was not seen in his proper depths: biologically he was a chemism of a bundle of nerves, sociologically and politically he was manpower and a product of his environment, historically he was a being experiencing and suffering history. At basis man became a reflex machine, an apparatus reacting to stimuli, without awareness of his innermost urge for experience and meaningfulness, for his self-stand. In the last twenty years, however, we see the outline of a new orientation toward the person. Disregarding certain very vague social and political tendencies toward the personalization of public life, we find coming to the fore, mainly from two directions, sincere efforts not only to give the human person his due but also to understand and emphasize him in his total significance.

First we see in many alert people today a very pronounced tendency toward a more personal formation of their existence. Through a more existential fulfillment of their life, for instance through "commitment," or through certain practices of meditation (and among these the yoga exercises, especially, play an important role), or through an individuation process as understood by depth psychology, these people seek to discover a way out of the shambles into an inner integrity. What they are looking for is an inner psychic center, a center from which the many complications of life's external relationships can be mastered and at the same time a personal sphere can be experienced which alone allows man to feel himself "realized" in his actual being. Depth psychology, the most important of these efforts, is certainly developing more and more in the direction of the person. No longer can it be suspected of being merely a psychology of instincts. By means of Jung's image-psychology of the archetypes it has recognized the multifaceted structure and orientation of the soul and has advanced to the meaning-discerning spirit. It speaks about a "self" that represents the embryonic, virtual center of the entire conscious and unconscious psychic life. The dasein-analytical investigations of Ludwig Binswanger, Medard Boss, and recently of Gion Condrau are also progressing toward what we call the authenticity of the person when they speak of man's ontological ground of existence.[1]

---

[1] Cf. Ludwig Binswanger, *Ausgewählte Vorträge und Aufsätze*, Bd. 1, 190–217; Medard Boss, *Psychoanalyse und Daseinsanalytik* (Bern: Huber, 1957) 57–74; Gion Condrau, *Daseinsanalytische Psychotherapie* (Bern: Huber, 1963), 39–48.

Finally, the "personalistic depth psychology" of Igor Caruso and his school is attempting not only to collect and deepen these tendencies but to ground them in its own way.[2] The necessary consequence of this further development of the image of man is that methods of analysis are becoming more subtle and more adapted. But even the Freudian renaissance, as we understand it, is a part of the same tendency in so far as it is not adhering to the mechanistic Freud in an inhibited regression but continues to develop the ingenious elasticity of his methods.

Equally conscious and intense is the striving for personal life-formation among the many who are newly concerned with Christianity, whether they are still outsiders or those who yearn for a deepening of the traditional Christian faith. Their tormenting question is no longer primarily: How can basic Christian truths be understood and defended by the intellect? Rather, it is: How will Christian teaching and Christian life change me in my personal depth if I accept it? How will my humanity, in feeling and in action and in relationship to community, become richer and more vital when I form my life in a consistently Christian way? Thus, faith is confronted in a different manner, no longer merely with the intellect and reason but with the total being-man. And even more, one gets the sense that faith is not primarily a system but a last, inner depth where a living encounter with God

---

[2] Cf. Igor Caruso, *Existential Psychology: From Analysis to Synthesis* (New York: Herder & Herder, 1964) and *Bios, Psyche, Person* (Freiburg: Alber, 1957).

and Christ is possible, an encounter in which the person knows that he is "summoned" and must give an answer in which he must speak from his deepest core. The various "movements" within the Catholic Church are an expression of this striving for the personalization of faith and religious practice. The liturgical movement, the biblical movement, the retreat movement are all moving toward this inward way that leads to the depths of a true person-encounter with God.

Since these ground swells so clearly indicate the beginnings of a new image of man which, in its integrity, and, above all, in its authenticity, supersedes the shrunken image of the past decades, we can rightly ask whether a meeting of the two realms, the depth psychological and the religious, would not result in valuable insights and possibilities.

NATURE AND PERSON

It is first necessary to move the conceptual content of our understanding of person out of the sphere of the abstract and into perceptible proximity. Even though the metaphysical concept of person is exempt from any psychological determination and psychic knowledge, still, in my opinion, we cannot avoid applying this concept also to relationships belonging to the realm of psychic experience. Right though it is to define the person as an individual, spiritual being and to emphasize the uniqueness and inexchangeability of this being-person, it is equally important to recognize that man—because he is a person,

and only in so far as he is a person—transgresses the
limits given him, since within the biological-physical
realm he is a "being of nature." As a being of nature
man, too, is subject to physical, biological, and psychic
types of lawfulness which constitute his apersonal realm
of being. As person, however, he is able not only to further develop these determinations but to tune them to
one another, to order them, and thus to orient himself
toward a goal. As person, man can take responsible control over the powers of his nature. He recognizes himself
as a spiritually conscious, and hence free, bearer and pos-
sessor of his nature. In this self-possession he has an inexchangeable center which allows him not only to take a
position in regard to himself but also to enter into an
inner relationship with another being like himself, a
"Thou." It is only then that man lives from a personal
center and experiences the same personal sphere in his
fellowman. Only there where man forms his own existence out of this personal core does he gain his authenticity and actualize his "existence."

Although, according to his being, man is person and
must increasingly unfold the being-person, he can also
live on an apersonal level or remain in a prepersonal
phase; he then misses his actual being-man and has to
suffer the consequences of his unauthenticity: unfulfill-
ment, mass-existence, the neurosis of ultimate meaninglessness, and, not infrequently, cynicism. Many live this
way today. They remain grown-up children who make
money in order to spend their life and have it a little
"nice." They put on airs and wish to be considered impor-

tant, if not in a successful profession then in their hobbies or at least in their general standard of life. Or course
they have their hard times, too, but suffering does not
make them forge ahead or become mature but forces
them into a kind of subdued realism with a touch of resignation, which, however, should not be confused with
maturity, since it has much more the flavor of a kind of
philistine and epicurean ideology. Their insecurity usually
becomes evident in their irony and sarcasm. Some of
them do not even desire to become persons; this would
mean responsibility. They like to remain beings of nature,
unconscious, spontaneous, at the spur of the moment. At
the end of Giraudoux's *Amphitryon*, Alomene asks Jupi-
ter for the "kiss of oblivion." (She had given herself to
him and had abandoned her husband to Leda—of course,
unconsciously at first.) She wishes to remain a child,
wishes to dwell in the paradise of mere naturalness.
Thus the conflict stays in the unconscious without being
worked out, a conflict that could be so salubrious for the
development of the person. Such individuals run around
the periphery of their life-circle, more and more ecstatically driven. Very rarely or never do they reach the
center of this circle; in fact, they shrink from it, for, not
without reason, they expect to find only a vacuum there.

Personal existence, however, is life in this center and
from this center as out of the "fullness of existence." Is
this fulfilled center identical with the spirit, as some wise
men have thought, or is it not rather that innermost center of energy in which spiritual and psychic, unconscious
and conscious streams of life-energy meet and unite?

After all, human life is as much nature as it is spirit. The person who lives out of his center does not give an unconditioned, free-floating answer from his spirit alone to the calls of the world and the calls of God. His answer continues to be within the sphere of nature, yet should be permeated by the personal tonus of spiritual freedom. Such personal being and acting is clearly a task of life which cannot be simply accomplished (for instance, by mere decisions of the will). It also demands the acceptance and formation of the natural layer. Thus the person is not an authority set over and against nature but is in the midst of and through nature.

PERSON AND CONSCIENCE

Invisible and intangible, our person is the innermost, hidden core of our being. It is an ultimate, mysterious depth, the existence of which we sense and feel rather than have immediately present. Therefore every individual who lives as person is a mystery and remains for others a book with seven seals; and so, in the best hours of his life, he is pregnant with the mystery of his becoming-person.

The mystery of being-person conceals man and makes him lonely in the midst of the human vortex, even in the quietness of a loving two-in-oneness. The being-person gives this loneliness substance, meaning, and happiness. Whoever tries to take these individuals merely the way he thinks he already knows them will always misunderstand them. Whenever the psychotherapist deals with an individual who lives as person or when he touches the innermost personal core of a patient, his own being-person is called forth and put on the scale. Why does this happen so seldom? Does the person not have an organ for making itself perceived and its claims known? Does person not mean that there is a voice irresistibly and imperturbably sounding through everything, through all layers and shells, through all defensive masks?[3] The "per-sonare" of this voice seems so essential for the inner center of man that the voice itself is designated as a sounding-through, as person. We also call this voice "conscience."

Despite the general agreement in regard to its existence, there are different opinions as to the nature and meaning of conscience.[4] To my mind it seems both right and useful to distinguish clearly the disposition of conscience from the act or decision of conscience. The disposition of conscience is, so to speak, the structure-given ground plan and the permanent basic order of human nature seen in its integrity. To this disposition belong primarily three dimensions which we will only briefly allude to. First is the dimension of the *intra-individual* sphere, which comprises all biologico-somatic, all psychic, and, very importantly, the spiritual dispositions of human nature. These dispositions also form the basic potential which, as a dynamic entelechy, has in view the structure

---

[3] We know that, according to newer philological investigations, the term *person* is not derived from *per-sonare*. But, since for centuries this derivation has been considered correct and meaningful, its use should be granted a certain legitimacy.

[4] Cf. *Das Gewissen*, Studies from the C. G. Jung-Institute (Zurich: Rascher, 1958) with contributions by E. Blum, E. Böhler, C. G. Jung, J. Rudin, H. Schär, R. I. Zwerblowsky, H. Zbinden.

of the ego-person as an integral, healthy, and ordered center and lays the foundation for the development of the value-person, since the natural disposition as self-generation constitutes a self-value. In the somatic, psychic, and spiritual "health conscience" man experiences whether he is living according to the value tendencies of his nature or whether he is neglecting them.

The second dimension, *social subjection* and accomplishment, expresses human nature's inner interlacement with and orientation toward the human community. Man is not a closed, windowless monad but a being who is open on all sides; this is why his instincts display more plasticity and variability than those of the animal kingdom. Now a social order becomes necessary, not, of course, in the sense that an alien conscience (for instance, conformity to prevalent moral interpretation) could contradict the personal conscience. It would be an unauthentic life if man began to live on the judgment and expectation of others. One of the greatest achievements of Freud's psychoanalysis was the discovery of the fatal role of the superego (the unauthentic conscience formed mainly by outside pressure). In opposition to today's tendencies to overemphasize the social character of human nature, Pope Pius XII rightly stated: "There exists in fact a defense, an esteem, a love, and a service of one's personal self which is not only justified but demanded by psychology and morality. It is a natural evidence and a lesson of the Christian faith. Our Lord taught: 'Thou shalt love thy neighbor as thyself' (Mark, 12:31). Christ, then proposes as the rule of love of neighbor charity towards oneself, not the contrary. Applied psychology would undervalue this reality if it were to describe all consideration of the ego as psychic inhibition, error, return to a state of former development, under the pretext that it is contrary to the natural altruism of the psychic being."[5] After all, the social character is merely one of the dimensions of human nature and should not overshadow the others. Only in so far as this dimension raises its voice of conscience in integrity and unity with the other dimensions is it not a countermovement against the authentic and individual natural conscience; only then it can and must make itself heard.

The third dimension of human nature is that of the *transcendent* relationship so clearly emphasized in some trends of depth psychology today. Carl Jung has already portrayed God as the greatest and most powerful archetype of the soul and has emphasized the concept of God as a "simply necessary psychological function of irrational nature."[6] Igor Caruso, the founder of personalistic depth psychology, proceeds from the fact that neurosis is almost always a fixation upon something relative, whereby the relative is absolutized. The liberation from such fixation is possible only when the actual absolute is also given as an object for the absolutizing tendency (of course, not in a purely intellectual but in a total way). Here again we

[5] Address of Pope Pius XII to the members of the Congress of Psychotherapy and Clinical Psychology, April 13, 1953.

[6] Jung, "The Psychology of the Unconscious" in *Two Essays on Analytical Psychology* (*Collected Works*, Bollingen Series XX [New York: Pantheon] vol. 7, 1953).

do not deal with something heteronomous imparted to man, but, rather, that which is most proper and most significant to him is experienced as the copy of an eternal primordial image toward which he must transcend.

The three dimensions together form the ground plan of the human person and all three time and again sound through the walls and barriers built up against them: The voice of the natural disposition becomes a voice of conscience and a voice of the person, in so far as this person strives for realization, for taking on form.

But the person shows himself in his uniqueness and autonomy only when he makes decisions of conscience and freely takes a stand in situations that are complicated and perhaps difficult to overview. The free act of decision is the intrinsic personal act. In it the person bears the full responsibility for his decision and its performance. In the freedom of this act the person experiences his highest engagement. Here he makes his own fate. The objective demand of the three-dimensional natural disposition is thus subjectivized, transformed into personal commitment—or else is rejected and excluded from this innermost sphere. This decision of conscience is not a subjective ambivalence or the expression of a momentaneous experience but grows out of an inner union with the natural disposition. Hence, it is both unfree and free. In it man stands toward himself, toward the objective order of his many-layered nature. He freely opens himself up as person to the demands of his nature. But since behind this nature and its structure stands the Creator, the personal-living man hears the voice of God in his conscience and in his decision of conscience obeys the will of the Creator. This judgment of the conscience is absolutely binding and constitutes thereby the freedom and dignity of the person against the ambivalent demands of human authorities. Being-person stands and falls with the conscience.

THE TASK

Hence being-person is not a pale and thin "metaphysical" matter but man's actual and necessary task of life. Granted, education has always intended to form responsible and free individuals; however, one cannot but feel that all too often it has forgotten the natural bases of being-man and thought it superfluous to listen to the voice of the individual conscience but instead has tried to drill in finished ideals with utmost speed. A true development of the person, based on the many new insights, will have to be more and more consciously aware of its possibilities and its limitations. All the results of the science of heredity, of the investigations of personality structure, of characterology, of the ecological sciences are part of the self-evident basis which can no longer be bypassed. Although it may seem impossible for the individual teacher or even the parents to appropriate and digest all these insights, they should at least be able to acquire a general knowledge which could help them avoid many mistakes and enable them to direct serious cases to the professional psychologist or educational specialist.

This holds true also for religious education and pastoral

care. Today we are well aware of the short-lived effects of mere religious conditioning and of passing on a proliferation of religious customs only for the sake of tradition. More important than man's incessant movement on the periphery of religion is the summons of his inner personal core. Christianity is the realization of a personal relationship with God, of a living encounter with him. Can the person hear this call and respond to it as person if he is not first "awakened" in his depths and is not as mature as the number of his years? In opposition to all this striving for a deep personalization of education and pastoral care, it can be argued from the religious standpoint that it is a fact of experience that a strong emphasis on the natural forces of the person can become an antagonism, even an unconscious defense against revealed religion. But is it not equally true that, if religion is to have its vital, strenthening, and productive effects on man and community, the natural dispositions for religious life formation are most important?

Redeemed and "begraced" nature does not become a puppet in the hand of God but preserves to a great degree its structure-given qualities, which need to be permeated by the person lest they become detrimental or destructive. Even if we remain aware that there are no infallible recipes for awakening a Christianity that consists of a living personal meeting of God and man, it will certainly be necessary to emphasize more clearly a personal attitude in one's religious life and to develop it more systematically. The development of the person toward maturity and responsibility demands a process of man's inner growth, which does not happen without the natural developmental phases and crises. Personal self-unfolding is therefore a necessary foundation and a natural precondition of religious maturation. Were this lacking in respect to religion, we would have to count on a constant miracle of grace, which God probably works only in exceptional cases. (And generally even in these cases the natural maturation must still take place; the example of Therese of Lisieux shows how much religious maturity also demands natural maturity.) Pastoral care, too, should therefore make use of all insights and aids for a more favorable development of the person. If depth psychology can offer such help, its collaboration with pastoral care becomes a pressing concern. Josef Goldbrunner has investigated these problems and has tried to show practical ways toward a fruitful collaboration.[7] As Goldbrunner rightly states, the danger of psychologism, feared by some, "cannot be overcome by rejecting the position of depth psychology but by making it a part of the structural order of the levels of being." Yet such participation presupposes a deep familiarity with the various theories and, above all, with the actual practice of depth psychology.

PERSON AND DEPTH PSYCHOLOGY

Through the *investigation of the unconscious* depth psychology has in general widened the field that is to be

---

[7] Josef Goldbrunner, *Cure of Mind, Cure of Soul* (Notre Dame, Ind.: University of Notre Dame Press, 1962). The same author published three small books *Teaching the Catholic Catechism* (New York: Herder & Herder, 1959–60), a practical application of the "personal method."

worked over and taken into possession by the person. Whenever this taking into possession occurs in a painful, analytic-synthetic integration process, man experiences the gradual disappearance of certain incomprehensible resistances, which up to then had continually thwarted his striving for an integral life formation. The unconscious parts of the soul which had previously led an opposing, independent life because they were not at all or not adequately joined to the conscious are elucidated and achieve a greater integration with this conscious. Persistent complexes, such as the positive and negative parental ties, are finally recognized and controlled. Lack of independence and submissiveness in feeling and desiring, in sensation and imagination are transformed into an adult self-stand and into the healthy self-confidence of a mature person. This enables the individual to respond more fully to the call of his conscience: Uncontrolled impulses grow weaker, compulsive tendencies toward instinctual compensatory reactions (for instance, the well-known power complexes, stubborn righteousness, intolerant aggression, and also the many inhibitions of some "pious people") lose something of their compulsive character. Incomprehensible contradictions in external behavior (kind-rude) become more balanced, and the unpredictability, so feared by others, is lessened.

This widening of the field of consciousness is not an addition of the unconscious realm of the soul to the conscious but is a fuller mutual permeation of both realms, resulting, according to Carl Jung, in the construction of the "self," which, so to speak, represents the psychic aspect of being-person. Naturally, the realm of responsibility grows larger. The progress of individuation gradually makes impossible the partial ethic of consciousness which dwells only in the lighted rooms of the soul giving no heed to its murky and dusty backrooms and, as a rule, "knows nothing" of the naïvely innocent and uninhibited injustices resulting from all too obvious projections of one's own dark side on one's fellowman. Thus a more integral self-discovery leads to a more comprehensive formation of conscience and allows one to comply more attentively with that which is personally recognized to be the concrete individual task of life.

In analysis the widening of the field of consciousness usually occurs in the grasping and *experiencing of symbols*. This experience not only widens the personal realm but leads simultaneously to a closer unity of the core of the person. The newly awakened understanding of the great world of symbols in the last twenty years is owing to the theoretical and, even more, the practical efforts of depth psychology. For more than five decades depth psychology has made these symbols the center of its methods of practice and, in the form of dream pictures and drawings, lets them become a strong and healing experience in the analysis. For too long the problem of instinct and spirit was seen only in its counterposition and was, therefore, considered as a purely ethical problem of will-attitude. A rationalistic approach apparently forgot the psychic bridge between instinct and spirit which is provided man in the world of images. The iconoclasm of enlightenment accomplished its purpose all too well. But, in consequence, man has been misunderstood in his

innermost nature and has been threatened in his becoming-person. After all, who, by a mere act of will, could
control his vital instincts for any length of time? The
anthropology of enlightenment ignored man's most mysterious and effective formative powers: the powers of im-
agery; and so, repressed and dammed up energies turned
into destructive forces. They attempted to assert themselves in the form of threatening dream phantoms and
in the not understood, derided artistic visions of expres-
sionism. Or else, through the proliferation of picture
magazines, they degenerated into simple, banal sensual
gratifications leveling all personal powers.

Depth psychology became extremely concerned and
emphasized the symbolic character of these despised and
mistreated images, not because of a scurrilous or snob-
bish interest but because of its experience with persons
under analysis. Then these images came into the foreground, sometimes as the expression of an inadequately
recognized inner situation or the neglect of vital spiritual
or psychic elemental needs and sometimes as the guiding
images of the task of integration and the way of individuation. While in the beginning this new evaluation of
images was quite insecure and was distorted by a hum-
drum, preconceived art of interpretation, in the course
of the last decades it has become much more precise and
differentiated and has moved out of a narrow naturalistic
ideology into the unbounded dimensions of the man's
soul. Therefore the experience of deeper meaning has
once more become possible, for the greatest and most
powerful of these images could not have come to man

from the exterior world but must have arisen from the innermost structure of his soul and sought to help this structure break through and take on form.

These images are the archetypes. Their discovery has rendered a valuable service to the building of the person. The consideration of these images as symbols can effect a better and more authentic union of the different psychic layers and powers beyond the integrity given by nature.[8] The image is the bearer of a psychic formative power, of a spiritual idea which, nevertheless, preserves its unbroken connection with the somatic sensate sphere. Thus it possesses a peculiar inner dynamic that makes it possible to introduce a process of transcendence which leads beyond the level of mere pleasure in the satisfaction of instincts to the plane of meaningfulness and value. In this way the danger of a dissociation of the person is eliminated and his centralization is furthered. At the same time man experiences himself as a being that realizes itself in a continuous process of transcendence. The image as symbol becomes the psychic transformer. Depth psychology has here recognized one of the deepest mysteries of man's becoming-person and tries to use it methodically to further this becoming.

Finally depth psychology advances directly and very persistently into the personal realm by mediating in the analysis the *concrete experience of person* and by creating a personal atmosphere. It is the person of the analyst with whom the analysand must examine his great prob-

[8] Cf. Jolande Jacobi, *Complex Archetype, Symbol in the Psychology of C. G. Jung* (New York: Pantheon, 1959).

lems in respect to their conformity with a greater reality and its authentic character. In the analytical process the personal questions of love and hate, of doubt and trust are uncovered, even in their final connections and backgrounds, and also are clarified in a common, great effort. Thus analysis necessarily involves a deep personal encounter. It is not at all exaggerated to say that there has never been a theoretical or practical science so intensely and deeply concerned for the individual as depth psychology. Even the great efforts of some schools dedicated to spiritual and religious awakening (for instance the various master-disciple relationships or that of the Yoga disciple to his Guru or Zen-master) generally do not reach the high degree of transference that is typical and necessary for analysis. The grand analysis touches the most intimate and hidden stirrings of the soul, man's weaknesses and failures but also his highest intentions and noblest longings. Man becomes transparent in his ultimate questionability and above all in his authenticity, honesty, and herewith a truly personal encounter, a kind of psychic partnership is realized. The person under analysis is allowed to be himself and feels himself accepted, not only as he still is but as he can and should be. The precondition for this experience with its person-constructing formative power is the true personal authenticity of the analyst, which is verified again and again in silence and in speaking, in passive and in active attitudes. In the psychotherapeutic analysis person grows through person.

We started with tendencies that show a distinctive direction toward the person. The less these tendencies

are artificially assimilated and furthered through preconceived theories, either naïve or reasoned, and the more
they really break out of the depth of the person himself
and try to assert themselves, the greater the possibility
that a truer image of man conforming to reality will
gradually be formed. The turn to a personalistic depth
psychology did not originate in doctrinaire deliberations.
Neither was it a necessary and self-evident result of experience with man in the analytical situation. Man cannot
be understood as simply a mechanism of reflexes and instinctual energy processes. He is not healed by the mere
disappearance of certain symptoms of organic and psychic neurosis. His psychic and psychosomatic constitution
in its plasticity points toward a center that not only
influences the somato-psychic events but should give
them an adequate and essential meaning. This center is
the person. Only when man lives out of this person-
center, only when personal life is consciously formed has
depth psychology and psychotherapy truly helped man:
It has led him to his authenticity.

PART TWO

CHAPTER VI

Religious Experience in the
Conscious and the Unconscious

Depth psychology is not an exact science in the sense
of physical science. It does not deal with exactly measur-
able quantities and magnitudes. The concept of energy
which it has long used and in part still continues to use
can be considered only as an analogy of the concept of
physical energy in its broadest sense. Neither is depth
psychology a science of the mind in the sense of Dilthey
and Spranger, even though the category of understanding
plays a great part in its endeavors. Rather, depth psychology stands between the two and, in some instances,
attempts to be a synthesis of both. It tries to find its material through exploration—hereby avoiding as much as
possible any kind of influence—through a free yet pur-
poseful gathering of expressions coming from the so-
called unconscious, and through the analysis of dreams
and drawings, it attempts to gradually order and understand this material. Yet its objective verifiability is difficult for one who is not repeatedly and newly convinced
of its correctness through the practice of this method.
Carl Jung stated in all honesty: "I have no theory of neu-

rosis." It may be even more surprising that he also did not have an immutable method. His statement is convincing: "I treat case x not according to Freud or Adler or Jung, but according to case x." However, we can say that probably all tendencies of depth psychology are guided in their work by certain basic ideas and anthropological models of thought.

When we say that psychotherapeutic depth psychology deals mainly with the neurotic individual, we must admit that the concept of neurosis can by no means be assumed to be unambiguous. But the fact that some insights and statements can claim validity even for the so-called "normal man"[1] and are thus of universal value for an anthropological psychology should have long ago been proved by its factual and important influence on this realm and on many other scientific disciplines.

One of the problems which has once more moved into the foreground through investigations of depth psychology is that of religion. Time and again the psychotherapist touches on the phenomenon of religion, and there is hardly any depth psychological direction that can bypass this phenomenon. The problem is many-layered. First there are religious questions which become active *through* analytical treatment: the religious compulsive neurosis (scrupulosity, irrational guilt feelings, etc.). It may also happen that religious problems awaken and become pressing only *during* the analysis: the problem of the inner discrepancy between dogmatic faith and per-

[1] Cf. Chapter I "The Normal Man."

sonal religious experience and, closely related to this, the problem of the discrepancy between an imposed standardized morality and a personal situation-ethics.[2] Here we shall point out a third basic problem of more general character, the problem of the opposition between the conscious and unconscious contents in respect to the religious experience. We shall deal both with its actuality and with the attempts that have been made to interpret it.

THE OPPOSITION BETWEEN THE CONSCIOUS AND THE UNCONSCIOUS

We will begin this discussion with two facts:

1. Not infrequently psychotherapy faces the fact that the conscious of the analysand displays a definite religious conviction while his unconscious has remained clearly areligious in its manifestations. This is not a matter of opposition between intellect and feeling, nor between a theoretical religious conviction and a piety of feeble experience, in the sense, for instance, so strikingly formulated by Fritz Leist, that one "can certainly have correct concepts of God without having a concept of God." Rather, it is a matter of a more deeply rooted antagonism. In the conscious, intellect and feeling may well go hand in hand and conscious religious experience can seem to be quite integral, while, nevertheless, there is a lack of inner integrity of the person since unconscious powers and tenden-

---

[2] Cf. Josef Rudin, "Psychotherapie und religiöse Problematik" in *Rettung des Menschlichen in unserer Zeit* (Stuttgart: Klett, 1961) 230–47; Josef Rudin, "Psychotherapie und religiöser Glaube" in *Neurose und Religion* (Olten: Walter, 1964) 63–94.

cies are opposed to this conscious attitude. As proof for this fact we refer to compulsive neuroses in the sexual area: cases of impotence, frigidity, fetishism, exhibitionism not infrequently found among individuals with a very conscious religious orientation and whose feeling life, also, has a religious resonance. Yet, more often in religious analysands we meet the most diverse forms of scarcely conscious aspirations to power, aggression, and hate feelings. Every psychotherapist is aware of this discrepancy between conscious religious ties and unconscious counterattacks, the compulsive character of which manifests itself above all through the exaggerated emotionality of these counterattacks. Wherever the inner antagonism is not conscious to the analysand himself, it reveals itself externally in compulsive symptoms (for instance, scrupulosity or in organic complaints: migraine, intestinal disorders, etc.), while the actual psychic problem is expressed in dreams and drawings. Let us give some concrete illustrations of this fact:

An extremely strict priest strives in his prayer for complete freedom from distraction and for a most intimate union with God. But time and again he experiences that in his very moments of greatest effort and most intensive prayer a voice comes from his interior saying a loud "no, no."

Another priest, scrupulous about his breviary, presents the following dreams:

"I am at a university. Everything is handled in a very scientific manner and every detail is paid attention to. I have already been reproached for an insignificant oversight of mine. All of a sudden guns are roaring from afar. They grow louder and louder. It becomes dark and frightening; the noise grows louder, and again and again fire flares into the sky. What has happened? An atomic war or the end of the world? In any case it is terrible and alarming. Nobody says a word; everybody looks out to save himself. I think of the end of the world and feel a certain joy as I say to myself: 'Now the time of science has passed. Now we will have another standard, namely piety and sanctity. Now it is the others who are worried and in fear.' I don't dislike this at all. In spite of the serious situation I experience joy, even malicious joy. After all, what can happen to me? What is going to happen to the professor, who is otherwise so smart?"

"I am coming from the church where I just finished saying Mass. Passing through a long corridor I come to the sacristy door. A sixteen-year-old boy opens the door for me and laughs very knowingly. His laugh seems to mean, 'I know why you need so much time to say Mass.' I become angry and box his ears. He gives me a long, strange stare."

Without going into the actual interpretation of these dreams as we do in the analysis, it is clear that both dreams point to a basic problem of this priest and that there are dangerous and aggressive tendencies in the unconscious of this otherwise very pious man: malicious joy at the very moment of the end of the world, anger immediately after Mass when he meets someone who intends to open for him the door to his inner problem, his self-righteousness: "Nothing can happen to me." Neither the malicious joy nor the uncontrolled attitude of anger fits into the conscious picture that this religious man has of himself and also shows to his fellow priests. They are in clear contradiction to this picture.

The discrepancy between the conscious and the unconscious of a religious person becomes even greater when *demonic* powers speak out from the unconscious. A woman patient writes: "I always have my worst dreams when I consciously and deliberately orient myself most sincerely and intensely toward God. They hit me like a slap in the face: It is useless; *this* is the way you are, and that's all there is to it." *Dream:* "Somewhere I saw the Walpurgis night, not in detail, but for a moment I felt the pleasure experienced on this witches' sabbath. I knew, or someone told me, that no one is admitted to this Walpurgis night unless he has previously made a pact with the devil. And though I did not see him, I already felt the evil one very close to me, standing in front of me. It gave me a feeling of vitality. But I did not want it, and I cried out and repeated aloud the name of Christ. All of a sudden I felt as if I were being choked and could no longer say 'Jesus Christ.'"

The same patient also had the "no" experience, similar to the first example. "The worst thing is that when I want to believe and trust in God with all my conscious energy, something in my utmost depth over and over again says 'no.' Time and again I discover despair deep down within me without my wanting it."

2. While the examples we have given illustrate how areligious forces break through into the religious conscious,

we also often meet the *contrary situation*. Individuals whose conscious life gives no sign of religiousness can suddenly be attacked by religious ideas and contents surging up from the unconscious. Religious tendencies break through and become manifest in dreams and drawings.

It is well-known that certain *conversions* are problematic. The psychology of conversion and reversion often leads us to ask: To what extent are conversions the result of thoroughly motivated insights, convictions, and free decisions of the whole person, and to what extent are they eruptions from the deep layers of the soul, which up to then had remained unnoticed and, consequently, generally discharge themselves with compulsive emotional force? What is behind the intolerance of so many converts, behind their hate of their former ways of life? Why their eagerness to make reforms even in the new community? Does the experience of conversion come only from above and from outside—or is it also an eruption from one's own inner unconscious into the conscious?

Such questions seem justifiable when we call to mind *similar events* in which the interpsychic functioning of scarcely recognized contents and ideas can hardly be ignored.

Mrs. M. is financially very well off but has no spiritual depth or religious orientation. She has a dream that she is going to a great feast. "On my way to the railway station I see an elderly man lying in the middle of the street in front of the railway station; he has apparently fainted. I hear him thinking: 'The party is going on over there in that house. Nobody knows that the feast is for me; I am paying for what they eat and for what they drink; the celebration is for me, but still they let me stay out here.' Nobody seems to notice the man; everyone passes him by."

She made the following association in regard to the dream: "For a long time I found nobody who resembled this man. Then a famous picture of a pope (perhaps one of Rubens') came to my mind. I think it was Pope Paul III, with a striking, oval face and an aquiline nose. Of late I have reproached myself at times because of the shallowness of my life. Perhaps the representative of Christ wishes to remind me with this dream where everything good comes from."

The same person had the following dream: "I am standing in front of an altar. All of a sudden I feel that someone (men are in the background) has thrown a great white mantle of gold brocade about me so that I look like a priest preparing to give benediction. Now I stand before the altar and begin to cry, since everybody seems to expect me to say Mass, which I don't know how to do, and besides I have no chalice. I wonder if I should say that I have the flu in order to have an excuse to get away. I wake up full of anxiety and bathed in perspiration. Is this not a religious summons to enact the mystery of transformation, which the dreamer cannot understand but which nevertheless gives her no rest?

With these examples we simply point to the fact that there is a frequent countertension between the conscious and the unconscious in respect to the religious contents. The material evidenced by this countertension can probably be confirmed by most therapists and supplemented without end. One can hardly go wrong in assuming that not only the analyzed patients but also the greater part of so-called "normal" individuals find a similar antago- nism between the conscious and the unconscious in re- gard to religion. In each case one part of the psyche seems to withdraw from religious influence, sometimes resulting in a resurgence of instinctual forces that degenerate and lead to perversions and aggression; while in other cases there is an urge for an ultimate meaning, for a union with the absolute, and for religious transformation lurking through the dark rooms of the soul and expressing itself in strange, incomprehensible, and even alarming images.

This leads to the obvious conclusion that the psyche of the neurotic person is not a uniform structure but clearly manifests the characteristics of dissociation even in respect to religion. Luther's opinion that man is rid- den either by God or the devil is proved to be incorrect, at least in the case of the neurotic, since he is simultane- ously ridden by both. But the neurotic is conscious of only one of them, while the other is a "ghost rider."

At this point the question arises: How should we interpret this countertension which can go so far as to become a dissociation?

ATTEMPTS AT INTERPRETATION

If we seek to go beyond the facts themselves and to come to an understanding of the material we have presented, various attempts at interpretation will have to be considered. These interpretations are certainly not answers and necessarily lead only to new questions. But it may be of value to sketch a few interpretative efforts so that we may recognize the multilayered character of the problem of the psyche and its religious involvement.

1. Let us take a prescientific look, so to speak, at the first fact (the conscious religious—unconscious areligious). Concerning this one says that it is a matter of "not yet," that the religious content is not yet adequately integrated into the unconscious, which still remains untouched by religion. At the same time one maintains that the contrary fact (the conscious areligious—unconscious religious) characterizes itself as a "still is," meaning that the religious content, *in spite of* massive secularization and religious indifference, is still deeply rooted and continues to be at least a latent residuum in the unconscious, from which it repeatedly cries out to be heard.

This interpretation seems to imply a contradiction, since in the first instance it is held that it is difficult to believe the religious leaven permeates the entire psychic structure, especially the unconscious, while in the second case the contrary is assumed without any hesitation and presupposes a deep-reaching and lasting penetration of unconscious layers. Or is this only a seeming contradiction, and could the two assumptions be coordinated with one another? It is plausible that the "still religious" points to a deep-rooted structural element, while the "not yet religious" indicates that this element is still undeveloped and not yet integrated within the whole person; this is perhaps the reason it can break through into the conscious in the form of dreams and at times even in an extraordinary way.

2. At first sight it seems more plausible to try to interpret the counterpositions of the conscious and unconscious according to the *theory of repression*. For if in the case of the "not yet" all concerns, doubts, and difficulties that are *opposed* to a conscious religious attitude are repressed, they dwell in the unconscious together with *suppressed* instincts and feelings and continually try to break out, whereas in the "still religious" the *religious* tendencies have been repressed and remain virulent.

Of course, if we base our interpretation on the mechanism of repression (with the phenomenon of compensation), we are faced with a rather serious problem as soon as we ask more precise questions. The most important question is this: In actuality, is there only one mechanism that works unconsciously, or is there not in most cases a half-conscious *suppression* which also somehow involves certain insights and freedom? For that which is repressed in the first place is the "embarrassing," the "unpleasant," the "improper." But that which is embarrassing, unpleasant, and improper in each specific case is defined by the superego, which is almost imperceptibly inculcated as guiding image and model in man through education and environment and one-sidedly demands the perfection of certain qualities. The repression of certain "improper" imaginations, feelings, thoughts, and urges almost necessarily involves an emotional absolutizing of those others which are demanded and fostered through education. Whatever does not seem to be compatible is repressed and pushed away into the id. Both the "wastebasket" of the id and the dominant image of the superego remain generally unconscious, so that man is to a great extent at the mercy of unconscious processes. We do not live so much as we are lived. Of course, between these unconscious forces of the id and the superego there is the ego which is conscious of itself. But it generally seems to be feeble and of little influence, almost like a plaything between the id and the superego. Yet, it does exist, and Freud actually wants to widen the sphere of influence of this conscious ego. "Where there was id let there be ego." But we are inclined to ask if this did not remain merely a wish to Freud, one which he himself hardly dared to believe in. For according to his theory, what finally prevails is the death instinct, which means that the conscious ego, too, can become an unconscious id. It is this *weakness* of the conscious ego which, according to Freud, allows the mechanism of his instincts to have great power over man. No matter how much Freud insists on these experiences, which again and again have been newly confirmed, the role of the ego cannot be completely reduced to a nothing.

The main problem of every theory regarding human instincts does not originate in the instincts themselves—which, by the way, we never find in a pure form—but in their more or less intimate connection with the *non*-instinctual components and especially in the degree of conscious control exercised by the ego over the instincts. The existence of the ego also necessarily poses the question of insight and freedom. A theory of instinct that seeks to explain all psychic events in an exclusively mechanistic way cannot bypass the fact that in the actual *practice* of therapy the instinctual model is not completely realized. Perhaps it could be validly confirmed if there were only the *id* and *superego*. But since an ego interposes itself and experiences itself consciously, the patients themselves refuse to accept it as only mechanism. Even on the theoretical level Freud had to admit that there "is no satisfactory doctrine of the instincts" and that the instincts are "mysterious forces." Testifying to his scientific honesty is the fact that he hypothetically established at least three theories of instincts, two of which represent a conscious instinct-dualism which was supposed to explain the dialectic of repression and dissociation. At first the opposition between the libidinal id-instincts and the preserving ego-drives were meant to do this. But since the ego-drives proved to be narcissistic-libidinal and suggested an instinct-*monism* with too little libido-impetus (second theory), Freud searched for a new contrast between the libidinal instincts and the destructive and death instincts in order to permit a better insight into the inner dissociation. His hesitation proves that he himself was by no means satisfied with these hypotheses.

The conception of religion as a compensation or an unconscious sublimation of libido points back to this instinctual mechanism. True enough, these transformations of instincts are clearly recognizable in many cases. But there are also cases in which the religious content, without ever becoming compulsive in character, continually prevails in a person's life and at the same time allows a healthy instinctual life. The causal-mechanistic interpretation of the countertension between the unconscious and the conscious is not completely satisfactory.

C. G. JUNG'S INTERPRETATION

Jung does not look for a merely causal explanation of this tension and possibility of dissociation of the psyche but seeks to understand it in a final sense. Yet such an understanding seems possible only if the opposites are put into a higher synthesis and can be experienced as the components of a greater wholeness. The conscious and unconscious are for Jung not two separate absolute principles but two complementary and coordinated fields of force oriented toward a goal. This goal does not seem to be within the field of force of the psyche itself. Thus, countertension does more than simply make possible the capacity for pleasure and work. The goal is not productivity but an integrated way of being.

For Jung the unconscious is not primarily a product of repression but a part of the being as it is, to which both the conscious and the unconscious belong, since it is not a pure spirit. As part of the being, the unconscious can never be completely transformed into the conscious. The conscious and the unconscious are seen as correlatives. The psyche itself is not primarily an energy field of the instincts but a system correlating the conscious and the unconscious. From this viewpoint both an obvious dissociation and a relatively good integration between the conscious and unconscious are possible. In certain phases of psychic development we meet a greater dominance of the unconscious, in other phases that of the conscious. But when it comes to an actual dissociation of the two, the danger of neurosis and even of psychosis seems unavoidable. Thus the task appears to be the realization of a better union of the conscious and the unconscious through the process of integration, without forming an indistinguishable fusion. Jung calls it the *process of individuation*. Its never completely attainable goal is the self as an always greater integrity of the conscious and unconscious. Yet this goal is not a final state that is speculatively thought out but a form of life that expresses itself ever anew and stirs up the psyche through images of experience. (Therefore it is incorrect to label Jung as a philosophical psychologist.) These images are symbols that show man the way to the "self."

According to its nature, the symbol is the expression of a union of psychic opposites (*sym-ballein*); what otherwise remains separate is, in the symbol, combined into a more complete wholeness and unity; instinct and spirit, feminine and masculine, knowledge and faith, temporal and supratemporal, finite and infinite.

The symbol is not only the expression of a greater wholeness, but it possesses an effective power proper to itself. As exemplar and model, as *causa exemplaris*, it possesses a dynamic force. This force urges toward the realization of wholeness and so toward an ever more complete overcoming of dissociation and split.

The *religious* symbol is of utmost importance. It unites

the human and the divine, so that it leads man beyond himself. Of course, it cannot represent the divine as such, since as psychic product it merely bears the character of a more complete wholeness and thus is not something absolutely divine and simply transcendent. Yet, often its qualities point clearly to the realm which men of the most different cultural levels have called religious, and its effect on those experiencing it is so overwhelming that it can hardly be denied the character of the numinous, in the sense of Rudolf Otto. Religion, for Jung, is "the attitude of the conscious which has been transformed through the experience of the numinous."[3] Unfortunately, we still lack thorough studies of Jung's concept of the numinous, but it seems that Jung is here arguing for a standpoint of value which lies beyond a purely energetical thinking.[4]

Needless to say, we deal here with a natural religiousness, immanently given and designed for man, and yet also demanded of him, and not with a revealed message in the sense of Christianity. The revelational character of Christianity is in no way touched, although the *anima naturaliter religiosa* can serve as a good disposition for this message and is probably even needed in most cases. Hence, the way of individuation is never a way toward redemption from sin (even from original sin), nor is it

[3] C. G. Jung, *Psychology and Religion* (*Collected Works*, Bollingen Series XX [New York: Pantheon] vol. 11, 1958) 8.

[4] Jung, "The Psychology of the Unconscious" in *Two Essays on Analytical Psychology* (*Collected Works*, Bollingen Series XX, vol. 7, 1953) 193.

a way to receive supernatural grace. It is a way of liberation from psychic obstacles, neurotic symptoms, and too great an opposition between the conscious and unconscious and, from the positive viewpoint, a way toward the unfolding and formation of the integral person on the natural level.

Every explanation of Jung's ideas is in danger of being formulated as a philosophical theorem or even as a system. Therefore it is necessary to emphasize that Jung's procedure was really just the reverse. He set out from experiences, from facts which confronted him in psychiatric and psychotherapeutic practice, and he searched for a satisfactory interpretation of these facts. Such an interpretation had to take into account the actual meaning of the material in question as well as man's naturally given disposition toward it. This material, consisting of dreams, phantasies, and drawings, often had no clearly definable symptomatic character but contained obvious indications of symbolic qualities. These symbols then had to be both interpreted in a final sense and inferentially reduced to a psychic background, since it was clear that, despite individual and cultural differences, certain symbols which had much in common turned up repeatedly. Out of this surprising discovery grew the postulate of the *archetype* which is rooted as disposition in the structure of the psyche itself and urgently seeks to be concretized in ever new symbol-formations.

Thus the archetypes have a serving function in that they are, so to speak, the dispositional frames for the symbolic formation of life-significant figures and processes.

However, to realize these formations (in symbols of art, religion, science, politics, and so forth), external factors must be favorable: the general cultural level, its understanding for and connection with such symbols. Whereever these preconditions are missing, the archetype does not remain passive but often has a negative and destructive effect. The neuroses of meaninglessness and inner emptiness, even of despair, result from such situations.

Concisely, one may say: For Jung the conscious and unconscious are part of man. They have a correlating function so that in the beginning the unconscious plays the role of a compensating power, of a natural complement to the conscious. If this role becomes impossible, the unconscious takes on the role of the opposition, of the adversary.

This explains Jung's interest in the "*mysterium coniunctionis*,"[5] in the union of opposites, the fertile tension-unity of intrapsychic polarities. Integration of ego and id into the self does not mean that the entire id can be integrated into the sphere of the conscious. As much as Jung likes to quote the apocryphal saying of Jesus: "Blessed are you for you know what you do," he says with the same conviction: "An adult must have enough honest self-criticism and humility to know where, and in which regard, he has to behave like a child, that is, as one irrationally and unreflectingly receiving."[6] In this

[5] Jung, *Mysterium Coniunctionis* (*Collected Works*, Bollingen Series XX, vol. 14, 1963).
[6] Jung, *Symbolik des Geistes* (Zurich: Rascher, 1948) 422.

consists the often misunderstood "acceptance of the shadow."

And the Experience?

Psychotherapeutic experience can confirm in many cases C. G. Jung's interpretation of the countertension between conscious and unconscious. A conspicuous attitude of the neurotic individual is that he rejects the union of opposites. He is adamant in his radical "either-or," and "all or nothing." Only with the greatest effort of thought and feeling is he able to acknowledge the simultaneity of opposites on a higher level. And it is only in the course of the analysis that his dreams and drawings finally show symbols of simultaneity, tolerance, and a new synthesis.

I recall a client of mine, a woman full of vitality, highly educated, and artistically sensitive, talented as a singer. She thought that the Church had a certain antagonism toward joy in life and disdained her sense of values. She had a dream that she was permitted to enter church in an evening gown in affirmation of her new-found joy in life. She even danced in the sanctuary. In her dream she recalled that King David danced before the Ark of the Covenant and that sacramental dances were common in the medieval period. Vitality and piety in no way exclude each other.

A later dream confirmed her in this new insight. She saw herself walking against the sun. This sun, of which she had also drawn a picture, was an enormous ball dominating everything. Its color was orange, which she mixed from a golden yellow (symbol of the divine sphere) and a fiery red (symbol of the vital sphere). The forces that had been threatening her fell down behind her in the form of very flat and pale flying saucers. In spite of their radioactive powers these saucers no longer represented any real danger to her.

Now let's take the dream of a Catholic priest. He says: "I am in Peru. I go to church and up into the choir so that I can watch more closely how things go on in Peru. The entrance music is really wild, and the faithful move rhythmically to and fro. The priest goes high above the altar to the pulpit with no railing around it. He preaches there without even getting dizzy. . . ."

When we recall that dreams often overfocus on something in order to make it more conscious, we understand that the wild music and the rhythmic motions of the faithful are a desire to express an intense and vital participation in the sublime mystery. And the fact that the preacher can speak without any railing around him (there are not too many infallible pronouncements today to lean upon), even without getting dizzy (is this dizziness of pride or fear?), should probably make the dreamer think about the meaning of an authentic and sincere sermon. Of course he can do this only when his pulpit is above the altar from which he receives the strength.

Certain therapists may maintain that these are examples of dreams of wish-fulfilment. We have no objection to this, if at the same time they admit that in them an inner authority yearns for the union of psychic forces felt to be in opposition and also works toward this union with the dynamics of the symbol, thus answering an existential problem of the individual undergoing analysis.

The dream symbol, from this point of view, indicates a model-solution. It becomes the *causa exemplaris* of a higher synthesis, and in some cases it even stimluates a new start for a more adequate solution of the religious problem of life. It unites the conscious religious ideas of the dreamer with the other aspects of the same sphere of experience which are still scarcely conscious to him. In this way a perhaps disturbing countertension between the conscious and unconscious in regard to the religious experience is elevated to a more productive level.

A careful summary of our explanations should yield the following conclusions:

1. The conception of the counterrelationship of the conscious and unconscious codetermines in general also the conception of the *psychic structure* of man. Although certain split-phenomena and automatisms could suggest that within the psyche there are two subjects or two systems[7] with the censor in between, the fact of a harmonious interplay, even a possible integration of split-off psychic parts, together with the fact of a limited but nevertheless effective control over "automatic" goings on and the well-founded opinion of the compensatory role of the unconscious seem to indicate that there is a unity and wholeness in the psyche, at least in the form of a *ground plan*.

2. The question of *meaning*, which seems to be coconstitutive of the conscious psychic act, is already presupposed

[7] Cf. Freud, *Gesammelte Werke*, Bd. X, 264–303.

through the mere *attempt* to interpret the opposition between the conscious and unconscious. It also seems not only justifiable but even valuable as a deliberately applied means of investigation. For Jung neurosis is "an illness of the soul which has not found its *meaning*."

3. In respect to the question of *religious experience* in general, we can consider Jung's thought as a rectilinear continuation of ten years of work in this field. At first W. James, T. Flournoy, and E. Starbuck declared *feeling* to be the only constitutive element of the religious experience, while Janet and Freud considered religious experience a pathological phenomenon. K. Girgensohn, W. Gruehn, and G. Wunderle discovered in this experience the wholeness of the psychic functions through the encounter with the wholeness of the "object."[8] Finally, Jung emphasized that the unconscious is also part of this wholeness; moreover, that in it the most basic dispositions are ready and waiting for their concrete configurations: the religious archetypes.

4. These explanations show that the countertension between the conscious and unconscious in respect to religious experience is of great importance, since it presses toward an ever greater authenticity and integrity of the soul.

[8] Josef Rudin, "Misstrauen gegen religiöse Erleben" in *Religion und Erlebnis* (Olten: Walter, 1963) 15–30.

CHAPTER VII

Answer to Job

TO C. G. JUNG'S BOOK OF THE SAME TITLE.[1]

Jung's sober and somewhat diffuse style picks up in tempo and fluency in this treatise and is continuously supported by an inner enthusiasm that, at times however, shows a strong trait of animosity which Jung generally cautions others against. He himself is aware of it: "Since I shall be dealing with numinous factors, my feeling is challenged quite as much as my intellect."[2] But this book has also provoked animosity among some critics who, because they are not sufficiently familiar with Jung's other works and with the entire development of depth psychology in the last decades, have felt inclined to view the *Answer to Job* as an erratic block, even as "petra

---

[1] Cf. in this context p. xi (Jung's letter to the author).
[2] Jung, *Answer to Job* (London: Routledge & Kegan Paul, 1954) xvii. "Answer to Job" is published in the United States as part of the *Collected Works of C. G. Jung*; Vol. 11: *Psychology and Religion: West and East*, translated by R. F. C. Hull. Bollingen Series XX, 11. Copyright 1958 by Bollingen Foundation, New York. Distributed by Princeton University Press.

scandali" in a realm which is normally that of theology. One could merely shake his head about such a work if he did not keep its basic approach in sight, especially since it shows little awareness of the enormous biblical-theological work of the last generations. Yet neither does it make such a claim. It seems only fair, therefore, that we undertake the difficult task of placing the *Answer to Job* in proper context in order to allow, in more correct though modest proportions, a clearer view of the spiritual value of this work. If we often let Jung speak for himself, we do so for reasons of a clean line of argument.

I THE BASIC THOUGHTS OF C. G. JUNG

The Situation of the Time and Jung's Answer to It

The *Answer to Job* is not a matter of new scientific results of Jung's psychology but an attempt to offer one more proof for investigations hitherto undertaken. However, the codetermining factor for the writing of this book was most probably the author's growing concern for the situation of our time and, concomitantly, his quiet hope of finding symptoms which he believed would lead to an understanding of this situation and thus create possibilities for a solution.

Jung is alarmed about developments in the world. He sees the enormous disproportion between technical progress and the attitude of mankind: "Everything now depends on man: immense power of destruction is given into his hand, and the question is whether he can resist the will to use it, and can temper his will with the spirit of love and wisdom" (p. 161). He speaks in this connection about the truly apocalyptical world situation: "Already the atom bomb hangs over us like the sword of Damocles, and behind that lurk the incomparably more terrible possibilities of chemical warfare, which would eclipse even the horrors described in the Apocalypse" (p. 146).

Even earlier Jung had similar thoughts, and in *Psychology and Alchemy*, a book whose importance for the development of Jung's psychology is as yet hardly sufficiently recognized, he wrote: "The great events of our world as planned and executed by man do not breathe the spirit of Christianity, but rather of unadorned paganism. These things originate in a psychic condition that has remained archaic and has not been even remotely touched by Christianity. . . . With the methods employed hitherto we have not succeeded in Christianizing the soul to the point where even the most elementary demands of Christian ethics can exert any decisive influence on the main concerns of the Christian European. The Christian missionary may preach the gospel to the poor naked heathen, but the spiritual heathens who populate Europe have as yet heard nothing of Christianity. . . . So long as religion is only faith and outward form, and the religious function is not experienced in our own souls, nothing of any importance has happened."[3] His *Aion* expresses similar thoughts.

[3] Jung, *Psychology and Alchemy* (*Collected Works*, Bollingen Series XX [New York: Pantheon] vol. 12, 1953) 11–12.

Jung's work and the *Answer to Job* are totally incomprehensible to anyone who misses this view of the contemporary situation and its deepest psychic problem which Jung has met in his practice for decades.

According to Jung, it is in view of this gloomy situation of our times that the dogma of Mary's assumption into heaven has been proclaimed. To him it is the "most important religious event since the Reformation" (*Answer to Job*, p. 169), and he sees herein something like the fulfillment of the vision of the Apocalypse, "the *sun-woman* 'with the moon under her feet [the symbols of the opposed forces of the cosmos and of the two sexes as well as of their union and, hence, wholeness] and on her head a crown of twelve stars.' [Apoc. 12:1] She was in the pangs of birth, and before her stood a great red dragon that wanted to devour her child" (p. 126).

Jung sees this dogma as an *answer* to the pressing problem of the times, an answer analogous with that which he himself has for years felt constrained to give in view of his psychological investigations and insights. It involves a new step in the "becoming-man" which psychologically is always due at the moment when the previously accepted way of being-man can no longer cope with the new problematic situation. Jung also calls these different phases of being-man the way of individuation, not because it leads to individualism but because it urges man to a greater and more comprehensive wholeness of his own being, in which also a part of the hitherto unconscious contents of his nature is honestly recognized and integrated. This is also the dominant theme of the book of Job:

"The only thing that really matters now is whether man can climb up to a higher moral level, to a higher plane of consciousness, in order to be equal to the super-human powers which the fallen angels have played into his hands. But he can make no progress with himself unless he becomes very much better acquainted with his own nature. Unfortunately, a terrifying ignorance prevails in this respect, and an equally great aversion to increasing the knowledge of his intrinsic character. However, in the most unexpected quarters nowadays we find people who can no longer blink the fact that something *ought* to be done with man in regard to his psychology. Unfortunately, the word 'ought' tells us that they do not know what to do, and do not know the way that leads to the goal" (*Answer to Job*, p. 163).

Jung finds the goal of the way of individuation designed in the "archetype of the self" which, as a stimulus for wholeness, dwells in the collective unconscious of man. It is not possible for us to go into detail here concerning the archetypes. In any case, Jung meets this archetype and its symbolism repeatedly in the course of the analytic-synthetic process. To a great extent the symbols of the self correspond to religious images and ideas, even to the objects and persons of the religious cults of various cultures: Buddha, Christ, and even the symbolism of the divine phenomenon itself (symbols of the Trinity, etc.). Does Jung intend to say that the true and total becoming-man in its deepest meaning is a becom-ing-God? And if so, in what sense? Jung simply answers that it is not his function as a psychologist to go into theological questions, just as in general he is always aware of being a layman "in *theologicis.*" *Empirically,* of course, the archetype of the self, which comes to the fore in the material of the unconscious, cannot be dis-tinguished from the images of God in the various reli-gions. According to Jung the process of a new becoming-man in the psychic sense depends essentially, both for the individual and for the collective situation, on whether this particular archetype of the self is recognized and gradually integrated. Only in this case will both the indi-vidual and the culture be able to work out their urgent problems, not merely one-sidedly but in an integrally correct and healthy way. Jung hereby in no way denies the importance of "grace," but as a psychologist his pri-mary task is to bring man to face his *own* responsibility:

"This involves man in a new responsibility. He can no longer wriggle out of it on the plea of his littleness and nothingness, for the dark God has slipped the atom bomb and chemical weapons into his hands and given him the power to empty out the apocalyptic vials of wrath on his fellow creatures. Since he has been granted an almost godlike power, he can no longer remain blind and unconscious" (p. 164).

The archetype of the self, the soul's integral God-image, must be formed, the new becoming-man must be realized. This is Jung's answer to the situation of the times.

The Meaning of the Book of Job

In this view of the contemporary situation and the task facing us, it is understandable that Jung has been examining historical documents of different cultures and religions for years in order to discover, even in the most startling statements and tendencies, intimations bespeaking the way of individuation, a true becoming-man. For this end Jung has accumulated an enormous amount of material.[4] The book of Job itself "serves as a paradigm for a certain experience of God which has a special significance for us today. These experiences come upon man from inside as well as from outside, and it is useless to interpret them rationalistically and thus weaken them by apotropaic means" (p. 4). This statement should always be kept in mind as we read the book. For afterwards Jung speaks almost exclusively about God, directly of Yahweh, just as in his discussions concerning the Apocalypse he speaks only of "Christ." With these terms Jung is *always* referring to the intrapsychic image and experience of these figures. He considers the book of Job not as a book of revelation, as the Church interprets it, but as a document of religious ideas and thus as a revelation of the soul: "In what follows I shall attempt just such a discussion, such a 'coming to terms' with certain religious traditions and ideas . . ." (p. xvii). "I would go a step further and say that the statements made in Holy

---

[4] Cf. Jung, *Psychology and Alchemy* (*Collected Works*, Bollingen Series XX, vol. 12, 1953); *Symbols of Transformation* (*Collected Works*, vol. 5, 1956); *Aion* (*Collected Works*, vol. 9, pt. 2, 1959), especially the chapter "Christ, a Symbol of the Self."

Scriptures are also utterances of the soul—even at the risk of being suspected of psychologism . . ." (p. xv). "How the people of the Old Testament felt about their God we know from the testimony of the Bible" (p. 3).

Thus Yahweh of the Old Testament is to be analyzed (just as Jung later analyzes the Christ of the Apocalypse) as a confrontation of the chosen people with their image of God. The results are at first crushing. The image of Yahweh reveals an archaic God. "Of course one must not tax an archaic god with the requirements of modern ethics" (p. 13). "His incalculable moods and devastating attacks of wrath had, however, been known from time immemorial" (p. 11). He is "amoral," since he beats even Job, the just, without reason; he is a God who "knew no moderation in his emotions and suffered precisely from this lack of moderation. . . . he was eaten up with rage and jealousy. . . . Insight existed along with obtuseness, loving-kindness along with cruelty" (p. 3). Satan can mislead Yahweh to a massive violation of his own penal code. He violates contracts and is so irreconcilable that he can be calmed only through human sacrifices and even allows his own son to be killed.

"Such a condition is only thinkable either when no reflecting consciousness is present at all, or when the capacity for reflection is very feeble and a more or less adventitious phenomenon. A condition of this sort can only be described as *amoral*" (p. 3). According to Jung this Yahweh merely manipulates his omnipotence and his arbitrariness and forgets to consult with his omniscience; in fact he even splits it off from himself. This means that the chosen people see their God as one intoxicated by his tremendous power, which blindly asserts itself even against better judgment and which, in spite of all contracts, allows the just Job and all humanity with him to suffer unjustly. Nevertheless the book of Job is a turning point. For this time the man Job proves morally superior to Yahweh. It could be that Job recognizes the weaknesses of Yahweh, that is, of the God-image of the times. It becomes evident that the hitherto accepted picture of God is inadequate and must be completed: Omnipotence and omniscience must be united with one another. Hence "God must integrate his repressed omniscience into his conscious self, he must become more human: "Yahweh must become man precisely because he has done man a wrong . . ." (p. 69). "This time it is not the world that is to be changed; rather it is God who intends to change his own nature" (p. 56). "He raises himself above his earlier primitive level of consciousness . . ." (p. 69).

Thus, according to Jung's thorough analysis, humanity's God-image must begin its way of individuation, the moment of becoming-man has arrived. This is the answer to Job: the becoming-man, the humanization of God through the consciousness of a deeper nature of God. Jung believes that shortly after the writing of the book of Job this humanization of God becomes clearly outlined in the Wisdom books, since now "Sophia" means the participation of God's omniscience and represents a prefiguration of Mary.

For Jung the becoming-man takes place in ever new

phases. A great phase was the becoming-man in Christ, who showed men the loving and kind Father-God. But this becoming-man remains somehow unsatisfactory, since Christ does not seem to be an empirical man. Because of his virgin birth he is a "hero and half-god in the classical sense" (p. 112). "The essential thing about the creaturely human being, sin, does not touch him" (p. 112). Christ is not a real man since too many precautions have been taken in order to avoid any interference of Satan in this becoming-man. Nevertheless, Christ's position as mediator remains significant; Christ is even the "answer to Job," above all in that sublime moment of deepest contemplation at the cross, in his cry of despair: " 'My God, my God, why hast thou forsaken me?' Here his human nature attains divinity; at that moment God experiences what it means to be a mortal man and drinks to the dregs what he made his faithful servant Job suffer" (p. 74).

Still his becoming-man cannot be fully successful, for Christ stands more on the divine side than on the human. Therefore a further becoming-man of God is necessary which, according to Jung, happens with the sending of the Holy Spirit. In this becoming-man God is "begotten in creaturely man" (p. 114). "The future indwelling of the Holy Ghost in man amounts to a continuing incarnation of God. Christ, as the begotten son of God and pre-existing mediator, is a first-born and a divine paradigm which will be followed by further incarnations of the Holy Ghost in the empirical man" (p. 114). The previously mentioned vision of the Apocalypse, the woman who gives birth to the divine man-child (there is no mention of a virgin), is considered by Jung to be the promise of a future becoming-man of God following the apocalyptic event.

We cannot enter more into detail here regarding the problems connected with the figure of Mary. To Jung the mother of Christ, because of her perpetual virginity and her immaculate conception is, so to speak, "elevated to the status of a goddess and consequently loses something of her humanity. . . . Both mother and son are not real human beings at all, but gods" (p. 58). The woman in the Apocalypse, however, is "not a goddess and not an eternal virgin. . . . She is the feminine Anthropos, the counterpart of the masculine principle. . . . symbolizes the hierogamy of opposites, and reconciles nature with spirit" (pp. 126–127).

Herewith Jung strives for the completion so emphasized by him as being the goal of psychic development and the overcoming of the manifold miseries of the times: the "answer to Job."

II OPEN QUESTIONS

Basics: Psychologism or Legitimate Approach?

What bothers and irritates many Christian readers is, first, the matter-of-fact attitude which Jung takes toward the revealed books of Judaism and Christianity in his psychological approach. They fear the danger of profaning and psychologizing the word of God. While they admit that this word must be perceived and worked out in the soul and must therefore take the psyche and its conditions into consideration, they emphasize just as clearly that it points beyond the individual psychic disposition and situation as a revelation of the transcendent God and, more precisely, not only in its origin but also in its ultimate meaning. Can psychology, then, be denied the right—granted not only to the history of religion but also to philosophy and even the natural sciences—of investigating these books according to its own methods and hereby cooperating in a deeper understanding of the revealed word's essential meaning? Would this not help us to more clearly distinguish this meaning from what is merely its literal and psychological clothing (which, as we know, corresponds to the specific cultural situation) and thus bring into focus the universally valid and supratemporal?[5]

Not without justification Jung once said: "In a series of reactions it became clear to me that occasionally my readers take offense at psychological discussions of Christian symbols, even though these discussions carefully avoid touching upon the religious value in any way. My critics would probably object less to the same psychological treatment of Buddhistic symbols, whose sacred-

[5] Therefore the psychology of religion of Girgensohn, Gruehn, Wunderle, and Mager have also been accepted by Catholic groups, since generally the religious and the mystical experience are also based upon the psychic structure, thus being accessible to the investigations of psychology. Cf. Mager, *Mystik als seelische Wirklichkeit* (1947); E. Raitz v. Frentz, "Das religiöse Erlebnis im psychologischen Laboratorium" in *Stimmen der Zeit*, Bd. 109, 200; Josef Rudin, *Religion und Erlebnis* (Olten: Walter, 1963) 15–30.

ness is equally unquestionable. Yet, sauce for the goose is sauce for the gander. I also seriously ask myself whether it would not be much more dangerous if Christian symbols were withdrawn from the intellectual grasp and moved into a sphere of inaccessible incomprehensibility. Too easily they become so remote that their irrationality turns into scandalizing meaninglessness. Faith is a charisma not given to everyone; therefore man has a mind that can strive for the highest things."[6]

This passage is noteworthy, for it shows once again that Jung is concerned for the religious "value" of the psychic experience rather than for the religious truth, which is not in his scope as psychologist. We should be able to understand this concern of psychology without naïvely confusing the truth of revelation with the "powers of this world" or even dissolving it in them. The archetypes and their symbols are for Jung the elements of the primitive revelation which the Creator gave to man along with his nature when he created him according to his image and likeness. The archetypes are also generally the precondition (whether conscious or unconscious) for the understanding and acceptance of the positive revelation of God. Jung does not speak of the direct revelation of God to man; this is the theologian's task. But what about Jung's psychologism? As we know, not only Christians but even materialistic thinkers reproach Jung with psychologism.

Against the latter Jung takes a very strong stand in his *Answer to Job*: "Owing to the undervaluation of the

[6] Jung, *Symbolik des Geistes* (Zurich: Rascher, 1948) 323–34.

psyche that everywhere prevails, every attempt at adequate psychological understanding is immediately suspected of psychologism. It is understandable that dogma must be protected from this danger. If, in physics, one seeks to explain the nature of light, nobody expects that as a result there will be no light. But in the case of psychology everybody believes that what it explains is explained away. However, I cannot expect that my particular deviationist point of view could be known in any competent quarter" (p. 168, n. 2).

"I do not underestimate the psyche in any respect whatsoever, nor do I imagine for a moment that psychic happenings vanish into thin air by being explained. Psychologism represents a still primitive mode of magical thinking, with the help of which one hopes to conjure the reality of the soul out of existence, in the manner of the 'Proktophantasmist' in *Faust*: 'Are you still here? Nay, it's a thing unheard. Vanish at once! We've said the enlightening word.' One would be very ill advised to identify me with such a childish standpoint. However, I have been asked so often whether I believe in the existence of God or not that I am somewhat concerned lest I be taken for an adherent of 'psychologism' far more commonly than I suspect" (pp. 168–169).

Here Jung is apparently attacking only those who limit reality to the realm of the physically determinable and not those who reproach him with psychologism because he reduces the metaphysical and metapsychic reality to something merely psychic or at least tries to interpret it merely psychologically. This latter reproach is much more serious to Jung. He attempted to answer it in earlier works: "Time and again I am faced with the misunder-standing that the psychological handling or explanation of God reduces itself into nothing but psychology. Yet, it is not dealing with God but with ideas of God, as I have emphasized time and again. There are people who have such ideas of God and create such images for themselves, and this certainly belongs to the realm of psychology."[7]

"It would be blasphemy to assert that God can mani-fest Himself everywhere save only in the human soul. Indeed the very intimacy of the relationship between God and the soul automatically precludes any devalua-tion of the latter. It would be going perhaps too far to speak of an affinity; but at all events the soul must con-tain in itself the faculty of relation to God, i.e., a corre-spondence, otherwise a connection could never come about. This correspondence is, in psychological terms, the archetype of the God-image."[8]

Jung wants to be understood in a similar way when he speaks about Christ and relates him to the "self": "There is no question of any intrusion into the sphere of metaphysics, i.e., of faith. The images of God and Christ which man's religious fantasy projects cannot avoid being anthropomorphic and are admitted to be so; hence they are capable of psychological elucidation like any other symbols."[9]

In view of such statements it is difficult to reproach

[7] *Symbolik des Geistes*, 394 n. 16.
[8] *Psychology and Alchemy*, 10–11.
[9] Jung, *Aion* (*Collected Works*, Bollingen Series XX, vol. 9, pt. 2, 1959) 67.

Jung with deliberate psychologism, even though at times we find statements which lead to misinterpretation. Fundamentally, even from the Christian standpoint, one will have to grant Jung the feasibility of his approach. It would be better, however, if on his part Jung were more considerate of the other spheres of reality, those of the physically and historically factual and also of the transcendent-divine. Although the religious assertions of Christianity are psychic cognitions and in the case of the individual Christian should often become much more so, they still rest on the fundamental religious assertion of the actual historicophysical existence of Christ and on the historically recorded witness of his physical resurrection from the dead without which "vain too is your faith" (1 Cor. 15:15). Hence, the revelations of the Old and New Testament have a significance that the "revelations" of other religions do not have. They are not merely expressions coming from the depth of the soul but messages from the outside, from God himself, and, as such, distinguish themselves even empirically from the symbols of the psychic archetypes—if not necessarily in their effects, in their historical actuality. Christ's life is therefore not only a universally valid, archetypal reality but above all also a historical reality, and Christ as well as his mother are empirical persons who are not to be seen only as psychic gestalts. All intrapsychic ideas of God, of Christ, of revelation, and of God's becoming-man are based on extrapsychic realities that give psychic existence a completion and an existential fulfillment in the metaphysical and metapsychical realms.

The revealed books of the Old and New Testament are accessible to and valuable for psychological research, since they are historical documents. Nevertheless, their primary character of divine inspiration and the revelation of partly historical and partly transcendent truths should not be lost. That is why these books demand deep respect of the Christian and a careful effort to clarify their meaning. Did Jung always live up to this demand? His tone sometimes seems too facile and flippant and his knowledge of biblical theology too skimpy. The book of Job, in particular, as seen from a theological view has a meaning that goes beyond all its literary accoutrements and represents as its theme the sustaining and also psychologically determining basic forces of existence, namely faith and confidence in God, even in the face of the world's greatest human and historical catastrophes. Nevertheless, Jung's interpretation is essentially valid.

Individuation as Answer to the Job-Question?

In the last section we acknowledged the legitimacy of psychology's attempt to consider the sacred books of Judaism and Christianity from its own viewpoint. Since, on the other hand, we believe the sciences should not contradict one another regarding essential questions, we must now investigate how much the answer of Jung's depth psychology and the answer of Christian theology agree or disagree. If we suppose that Jung is correct in his conviction that the contemporary situation is comparable to the Job-situation and that Jung reaches the central question of the book, the problem still remains as to how far his answer is adequate for conquering world misery and suffering. Does his way of individuation gradually eliminate the cause of evil and lead mankind to that higher level where the naked striving for power, in general and in particular, can be controlled by a deeper wisdom and true love?

We could answer this question in the affirmative if the evil in the world were caused only by the psychic deficiency of man, by his lack of development, and, especially, by his lack of integration. But, as important as the role of these psychic causes is—and it is much more decisive than we usually suppose—this psychic failure is not the only, not even the paramount root of the evil. Christian philosophy still gives first place to a *malum* "*metaphysicum*" which necessarily accompanies the limitation of our nature and of the entire world. Our world is not the most perfect creation conceivable; neither is man destined by nature to reach perfection without suffering. Therefore time and again there will be situations with which human reason and goodness cannot cope. Yet, even if we accept this Christian interpretation of the roots of evil and suffering in the world, psychic integration, the "becoming-man" in the sense of Jung, should be taken very seriously.

The Christian approach in the truest sense, however, emphasizes two other sources of evil. One is the fully conscious misuse of personal power which so often causes deep misery and is perhaps responsible for many a world catastrophe. In this conscious failure, the unconscious deficiencies and imbalances do not play a determining role, and so a psychology of the unconscious cannot be of significant help. Rather, through a free decision man must again accept the disturbed order and freely orientate himself to it. Finally, as Christians we must acknowledge "original sin" as the first cause of evil and as the freely willed apostasy of mankind from God, whereby man has been deprived of the earlier relationship with the transcendent Creator. According to Christian teaching original sin cannot be reversed by man. The amelioration of the human situation depends preeminantly on the extrapsychic God speaking a new Yes to man. This has happened in the becoming-man of the Logos, an act that was not necessary, although psychologically meaningful and, most important, freely willed by God. The gospel demonstrates that this is not a "paying off of God's debt to man" and even less an "irreconcilable act of revenge of Yahweh, who in his anger allows his own son to be killed," but just the contrary, namely God's supreme act of love: "In this we have come to know his love, that he laid down his life for us" (1 John 3:16). In God's becoming-man there is no interplay of psychic mechanisms, no law of psychic energetics at work. It is rather a manifestation of freedom in its highest expression: love. This love of God is the final answer to Job and to the Job-situation of mankind.

Therefore, despite its importance, Jung's answer to Job is incomplete. Moreover, it is not the answer which the book of Job itself seeks to give. For in it is manifested steadfast faith acknowledging only one answer: that in all trials God is greater than man, the one whom we cannot teach (Job 21:22). Though we are convinced of the validity of the psychological God-image of the Old and New Testament—even of its fruitfulness—we should never forget that this God-image necessarily goes beyond all human dimensions and supersedes all psychic archetypes. The very purpose of the book of Job is to show this greatness of God and the corresponding human answer to it.

CHAPTER VIII

The Neuroticized God-Image

The modern era has once more become aware of the power of the image. Following the drought of an over-worked, bloodless rationalism, the hunger for the concrete has newly awakened. Abstract concepts may be more precise, more accurate and, above all, more convenient, but only images adhere to the soul and preserve their effects long after brilliant trains of thought have been forgotten. Therefore images can set the destiny of the individual as well as entire communities and cultures.

There are especially great, overwhelming dominant images that possess a molding power. They seem to enter our psychic realm not so much through the gates of the external senses but rather arise out of one's own depth and press toward personal life-formation. In the form of ideals ("This is the way I see marriage"; "This is the ideal of my life") or as models ("This is the way my parents did it"), dominant images can fashion and form life in its very details. Depth psychology speaks of archetypes, which as concrete symbols continually reappear in new guises, and yet their basic origin lies in the structure of

155

the soul itself, so that in the constant symbolic recon-
figurations what is essential to human nature becomes
incarnated and only thus takes on form. We may meet
such archetypal figures in the form of great works of art
or they may stir up our soul as primordial gestures and
utterances. They may speak in the silent works of nature
about the glory of creation's morning or in the unleashed
elements warning of the end of the world. They always
open up the bottom layer of the soul which seems to
be waiting in urgent readiness to form itself and to be
formed through such images and to learn from them the
meaning of the world and life.

The highest symbols connect man with the final contexts and relate his life to the supraworld, to God himself.
The God-image has been for thousands of years the most
powerful archetype, the most hidden energy center by
which ultimately all areas of life are formed. It is that
psychic position in which libido must necessarily be most
concentrated if human life, in the long run, is to remain
healthy and find meaning in profession, in marriage, and
in service to state and culture. In short, the God-image is
the most secret center of human existence, for according
to this image man seems to be created. Therefore time
and again he must find this image in his innermost self
and in all things and must be formed by it. Yet at the
same time the God-image becomes the most dangerous
consort of human existence. What happens when this
image is distorted? When it has repulsive, inhuman, neurotic, or even demonic traits? Must we then not speak of
a sick God-image disfiguring and distorting the soul? If
an authentic and true God-image radiates the powers of

healthy human formation, is a distorted image of God not, conversely, a source of dissolving, dissociating, and decomposing powers or of tendencies toward inhibitions and rigidities which cause an unproductive rhythm of life and a reduced, lopsided image of man? The significance and importance of this question demands more discussion. In the following we shall pursue three trains of thought which interconnect and complement one another since they rotate around the same center. These three are the fact, the manifestations, and the backgrounds of the sick God-image.

I THE FACT OF THE SICK GOD-IMAGE

Before we deal with the different manifestations of the sick God-image, we must try to find the *fact* of the distortion of this image by investigating the psychic illnesses which particularly involve the God-image and are constantly newly caused and intensified by this image. Here we refer to conditions known as religious anxiety neurosis, compulsive neurosis, and schizophrenic symptoms (without becoming fully psychotic). According to the understanding of modern science, at work behind these conditions are psychic complexes loaded with energy resulting from childhood traumas, fateful circumstances, professional and marital difficulties. These complexes often center around religious ideas or at least are intensified by such ideas. In the latter case the God-image plays an important role as nucleus or crystallization point of the complex process.

When speaking of religious *anxiety* neurosis, we do

not mean the dull and heavy anxiety feelings concerning the numinous which can suddenly come upon any alert person. We are not referring to the fact that individuals with a delicate sensorium for the suprasensual and the absolute may suffer from God because of their distance from him, because they cannot see and perceive him since he is the incomprehensible, the mysterious, the "totally other." We can call the Augustinian restlessness of heart a kind of primordial neurosis, but we cannot overlook the fact that since the loss of the paradise it is part of being-man and should not be confused with true religious neurosis. The inner upheaval, too, which through ascetic restraints or ecstatic submersions attempts to ascend to the heights or descend to the depths of God should not be generally referred to as exaggerated, abnormal, and neurotic, since it corresponds to a more essential understanding of existence and can lead to a healthier state. One does not have to be an enthusiastic Christian to share in the experience of man's God-problem and God-need. Nietzsche's terrible struggle over God did not necessarily have to end in his night of madness, and Rilke's circling around God, "around the age-old tower," should not be interpreted as only narcissistic self-reflection. Certain pedagogics are far from even sensing this restless process of searching for God. All this must be emphasized before we begin our discussion of religious anxiety neuroses.

The dread of God should also not be confused with the "fear of God" that is the beginning of all wisdom. The fear of God is aware of the absolute distance between Creator and creature. Therefore it turns into a reverence that bends down and, as a result, inwardly opens up and widens, hearing and listening to the voice of the higher and ready for devotion. But dread constricts rather than expands; it closes man up in a narrow pass (*angustiae*). Dread makes man incapable of a clear vision and attentive listening, and it hounds him through the labyrinth of his own dark passages. Dread puts man's very existence in danger so that he can find no way out. In such situations short circuits occur. Man finds himself in a terrible emotional turmoil, in a whirlwind of feelings and moods, of contradictory ideas and affects which can also be discharged in outward explosions and often manifest themselves in physical symptoms (trembling, shaking, etc.). Or it becomes a psychic death reflex, an interior and exterior muteness, a state of stupor and numbness, an internal and external blocking and freezing even to the point of a partial paralysis. In religious anxiety neurosis it is not infrequently the God-image itself that draws one into such whirlpools of anxiety or leads to such paralyzing states—a God-image whose profile is the cause of such manifestations of anxiety.

We should not be too quick either in settling on religious *compulsive neurosis*. In addition to its excellent insight into psychic contexts and inner dynamics, depth psychology should cultivate the more subtle distinctions of the individual phenomena. Above all, one should distinguish clearly between psychic compulsion and the feeling and consciousness of an inner sense of obligation. Obligation following from commandments and prohi-

160 *Psychotherapy and Religion*

bitions presupposes the freedom of man. Only he who is
in possession and relatively good control of his psychic
functions has the competence and sound judgment necessary for truly ethical behavior. Psychic compulsion, however, means a reduction and in some cases a considerable
elimination or even the total loss of this control and freedom. Whenever man acts through compulsion he falls
back into prepersonal behavior, and his gestures and
tone of voice take on a mechanical, automatic, and robotlike character. This leads to a sharpening of the external
forms of expression, often to a rigidity: The voice becomes hard and impersonal, the facial expression set,
masklike, all his movements seem stylized and lack the
human warmth and wonderful elasticity of a personal
and vital freedom. It is as though compulsive ideas and
impulses were flowing autonomously out of a single force
that has run amok and broken away from the psychic
whole, and they have been unleashed to inundate one's
own (often one's alien) humanity. The compulsive neurotic coerces himself and his fellowmen, and if he is a
religious compulsive neurotic he also coerces God: "He
must help me"— "He must give me grace"—"He cannot
allow this." Compulsive stereotyped repetitions, automatic use of magical prayer formulas, intolerant self-
torment, compulsive ideas of eternal punishment in hell,
or an imperative and constant compulsion to go to confession forces a first impression that the God-image of
this individual bears traits different from those of the
God of the Good News.

The fact that every neurosis reveals a loss of reality

points to the actual backgrounds of the neurotic process. For the reduction of reality is caused by the repression of life-significant questions or by a one-sided outer and inner way of life. A piece of reality that should have been lived or suffered through is instead submerged into the unconscious; or for some reason a decisive developmental phase has been avoided and psychic functions have remained underdeveloped. Through such conscious and, more often, unconscious "failures," a part of reality is split off from conscious life and condemned to a miserable existence in the unconscious. A *dissociation* between conscious and unconscious life takes place which, due to the compensation dynamics so characteristic of the unconscious, pushes toward a psychic fragmentation, contradictory behavior, even incomprehensible inverse experiences and attitudes. This inner dissociation should not be confused with that fertile psychic polarity, that tension-span which can encompass very different and contrasting psychic contents, feelings, and powers and unite them in a productive tension-union. Neurotic dissociation means that at times one group of psychic powers becomes independent and autonomous and at other times the opposite inner tendencies erupt and become the compulsive imperative. In the religious neurosis this dissociation manifests itself not infrequently as a compulsive hatred of God which arises from the unconscious, while at the same time there is a conscious striving to love God and be united with him. It seems as though in the God-image itself there is an inner cleavage, as though two incompatible faces turn the God-image into a Janus head. Anxiety, compulsion, and dissociation fit together into an evil triad; they interlock even in the religious neurosis. They force us to ask, what is this God-image that causes and furthers these neurotic symptoms and hounds man in a real diabolical circle?

II THE VARIOUS MANIFESTATIONS OF THE SICK GOD-IMAGE

The God-image of ageless traditions as well as that of Christianity is one of enormous inner fullness and infinite riches. Whatever magnificence and greatness is offered us through creation must already be within the Creator as its origin and original picture. Small wonder that such an original picture gives the impression of a gigantic mosaic which, in spite of all inner unity and integrity, is composed of thousands of little mosaics. It seems to be a *complexio oppositorum*, as theologians call it. God is simultaneously the one transcendently most distant and immanently most near to us; he is the great silent one and yet speaks to us in all things; he is the all-holy and still allows all the atrocities and the horrible crimes of humanity; he is the inexorably just and yet the most merciful. Incomprehensible, mysterious, enigmatic, he is the nameless of a thousand names. What theology calls the union of opposites is interpreted by Rudolf Otto, in his psychology of comparative religion, as a simultaneity of the *tremendum* and *fascinosum* in the numinous. He quotes Augustine's famous statement: *"Exhorresco in quantum dissimilis, inardesco in quantum simi-*

lis." Whether the approach to the nature of God be that of the philosophers with their dialectical opposites and paradoxes, or that of the poets with their courageous picture-language, or that of the painters with their palette of many colors, the salient counterexpression is always valid:

> "We build images in front of you, like walls,
> And, yes, already a thousand walls stand round you.
> For our pious hands conceal you
> Whenever our hearts see you open." (Rilke)

It is surprising that such a tension-charged God-image can become, in its magnitude and boundlessness, the cause of one-sided concepts, false ideas, misunderstandings, and misinterpretations. If we add to this the limited possibilities of human expression and concept formation and especially the fact that there is no symbol of representational art which can begin to approximate the image of the pure spirit of God, we can somehow understand Judaism's prohibition of images: "You shall not carve idols for yourselves in the shape of anything." It can not only become an idol, a fetish, but can also awaken and further false concepts of God. True, the iconoclasms of the Occident drove man into an inhuman solitude without images, but aside from their fanatic components, their positive influence should not be overlooked.

This is the necessary foundation for seeing the manifestations of a sick God-image in a right light. We can distinguish five groups of manifestations. In the first, the God-image is based on but a single dogma. For instance,

God is experienced merely as the absolute ruler. Then he is seen as a God of arbitrariness, an inhuman tyrant who cold-bloodedly predestines some to eternal damnation while he gives his favors to others for no reason at all: the *rex tremendae majestatis*. Or God becomes the distant inaccessible, enthroned in eternal majesty, with no care for the inferior human race which has been capriciously thrown into existence; or the God-image is persistently anthropomorphized into the long-bearded good papa in heaven, a jovial philistine about whom even the indifferent can say: "From time to time I'd like to see the old man." Or God becomes the correct business partner to whom one pays the "assessed tax" but who is not allowed to take a further look into one's books. Or it is the God-image of a dynamic pantheism that knows God only as the eternally becoming, as the one who ought to be, who always strives to take on form but who in no way can authoritatively demand and effectively realize it.

In the second group we can count the one-sided *moralizing* God-image. Here we have the rigid God of the law who minutely and revengefully guards the observance of his commandments. Most important for this God are red tape and formal juridical viewpoints. Woe to the one who would hurt or offend him, to childish thoughtlessness, or to the weak failure of one caught in imperfection! His vengeance is terrible. Compared to this touchy God, a revengeful wife is a thousand times more tolerable. He is the fussy bookkeeper God who pedantically and grouchily sits over men's books of life, making his entries of debit and credit and recording his merciless account: *"Liber scriptus proferetur, in quo totum continetur, unde mundus judicetur."*

In the third group we find the *secularized* God-image that transposes the absolutizing attributes of God into the realm of the finite. Herewith it causes a truly fatal confusion and raises hopes which necessarily have to be disappointed. As a result, compulsive ideas and dissociations are to be expected. Divine omnipotence is transferred to the state or to leaders, God's omniscience attributed to science (superstition in science, even in theological science, is by no means obsolete). God's all-goodness is traduced into mere humaneness, his infinity changed into idealistic progress, his fullness of life idolized as simple vitality. (In the course of this secularization other religious ideas, too, change their name: Paradise is located in a ski-resort or even in Hawaii, and hell seems to come to life in the concentration and labor camps of the demonic phantasy of a Brughel.)

It is only a short step to the fourth and fifth groups with their *magic* and *demonic* God-images. Here the attributes of God are not only projected into the finite but appear incarnated in these limited configurations and are charged with magic powers. The newest techniques place unlimited power over life and death at man's disposal, even to the point of the artificial generation of man. Psychic processes which dwell in the background can be discovered by means of today's methods of soul exposure, through a combination of test methods, or by use of the "truth-drug." Technicians, physicians, and psychologists achieve something of the image of a magic savior and practically usurp certain traits of the God-image. As a consequence even demonic characteristics come into play. "White magic" can almost suddenly turn into "black magic" and appear as the incorporation of evil itself. The God-image takes on the dimensions of something terrible, unpredictable, abysmal, and insidious, with cruel and malicious traits. In these instances ideas become prevailingly compulsive and an ultimage threat to one's existence. Then it is not surprising that suddenly bizarre animals and legendary monsters make their appearance with characteristics of the absolute: the dragon who spits out his deadly venom as he guards the hoarded treasure, the cat with panther eyes playing its game of cat and mouse with people, and the inevitable shining serpent that lurks in the rocks awaiting the victim of its strangling grip. Is it only incidental that these images play an overwhelming role in the dreams of neurotics—and that, in the method of free association, these images almost effortlessly and naturally come to the fore as associations of the God-image? These externalized forms of the neuroticized God-image are certainly not the exception, and with religious persons they can frequently even be compulsive. How does such an apparently demonic God-image develop? What psychic experiences, processes, and interconnections participate in the origin of these images?

III THE BACKGROUNDS OF THE SICK GOD-IMAGE

The investigation and illumination of the backgrounds of a sick, neuroticized God-image is one of the most diffi-

cult tasks. Man is here questioned in his total inner attitude, in his total development, with his most hidden
psychic wishes, stirrings, and motives. Feelings and ideas,
totally or partly unknown to himself, about which his
consciousness knows nothing, must be taken out of the
unconscious and laid open despite manifold resistances.
Thus every case is unique in its kind. Nevertheless, there
are perhaps a few common backgrounds in many of these
sick God-images.

First we have to consider the *transmission* of a
one-sided, mutilated God-image. All religious teaching,
whether instruction or sermon, faces the danger of pre-
senting a figure of God that is "stylized" according to a
specific section or even a single word of Holy Scripture,
so that seldom is an integral God-image formed in one's
inner polarity. Depending upon the individual's precon-
ditioning, it may be that at times the listener perceives
and retains only one trait upon which he becomes almost
fixated. Similar effects, of course, may be produced by
paintings and statues which, for instance in an exagger-
atedly expressionistic way, fascinatingly represent a single
aspect of the God-image. From this viewpoint one can
understand the necessity of the church's guardianship
over symbols and their formation. But, most of all, there
are the religious emotional experiences which the child
and the adolescent, still in the womb of their own family,
take into themselves by way of a natural transference.
Here, however, we must call to mind the profound analytical fact of experience that, surprisingly enough, children live the unconscious of their parents and educators
—in other words, not the God-image consciously pre-

sented to them but that which has been repressed and which therefore has an all the more uncontrollable effect from the unconscious.

In such cases anxiety motives and guilt feelings which are merely repressed produce their results and participate in the formation of the God-image to such an extent that they play a dominant role in forming the emotional attitude of the children toward God. This recognition makes it easier to understand why children are often afraid of God and why adolescents turn away from religion even though, or perhaps because, their parents had developed a very strong external religious behavior (which, however, was basically a form of fear appeasement). And, on the other hand, there are adolescents who seek their way to God despite the fact that their parents had banned all religion from their personal and family life. The transmission of the God-image is a very difficult problem and demands of the educators themselves a relatively good communication between their conscious and unconscious psychic life.

Clearly connected with this background of a sick God-image is, as a further neuroticizing factor, the *discrepancy* between the transmitted and the personally experienced God-image. We know how often a God-image is transmitted and also accepted in an almost externally mechanical way without leading to an inner assimilation. One's individual faculties do not participate in this process, and a personal experience of God, an inner experience, cannot take place. Thus the interior has ideas and rules of action that are completely different from those of the exterior: Conceptually a Christian God-image has been ingested by way of instruction and environment, while in the depths of the soul a pagan, gnostic, Manichean, magical, or secularized God-image is at work. In this case, too, educators must ask themselves whether their transmission of the God-image was, perhaps, so conceptually abstract that a psychic integration, a true and integral experience of this image, became impossible. Of course, it may also be that, because of the general rationalistic attitude of an era or of an instructional method, the capacity for experience as such remained undeveloped and, hence, neither could it be formed in the religious realm. This is a double disadvantage for a God-image that is so highly differentiated as is the Christian, since it means that from the very start an inner resonance and a personal experience become almost impossible.

An actual breakdown of a hitherto cherished God-image does not occur when, out of a great idealism, this image is venerated and in its perfection represents a model which is emulated in a modest sense of creaturely distance; but a breakdown does occur where this model is a compulsive idea with which one seeks to identify and which makes extremely difficult demands beyond one's immediate capability of realization in the concrete. Here an individual can be driven into a spiral of exaggerated demands on himself, of self-tormenting coercions and depressing inferiority feelings. A psychic breakdown is to be expected, and it often happens that, as a consequence, such a threatening God-image is liquidated and burned away, first as a phantastic idea but also frequently as a primordial image corresponding to nature. The God-image can then reappear in the form of a monster—for in one's interior, which had been identified with this image, the dragon or the cat comes to the fore. But the divine dragon is destroying. In this connection depth psychology either refers with Freud to the "construction of a superego" that by necessity must find itself in opposition to all realities or, in line with many newer approaches, speaks of "perfectionism" which thrusts the individual into the compulsive spiral.[1] Behind the concepts of super-ego and perfectionism are the mechanisms of identification and projection, well-known to psychotherapy, in which the God-image also plays a great affective role. Even personal failure and no longer deniable weaknesses are then finally projected onto the God-image or at least drive one to make accusations against a God who allows such things to happen. The entire problem of evil is projected onto the image of God: Age-old gnostic speculations once more become virulent and carry out their mischief.

C. G. Jung's psychology has placed stress on a wider background of neuroticized God-images: the separation of individual life and also of the conscious collective-situation from the archetypal ground-roots, the lack of a living contact between the conscious God-image and the unconscious *archetype of God*. In these cases the God-image has become too conceptually abstract, a rational skeleton, a dry, bloodless mummy. Everything numinous

---

[1] Cf. Chapter X: "Neurosis—Perfectionism—Piety."

is eliminated from it; it can neither truly and inspiration-
ally fascinate nor awaken a holy trembling within the
soul; it seems to be like a jointed doll which, according
to the feelings and mood of the moment, can be made
to move or be pulled out of joint, can become one moment the "dear God" and the next moment the dangerous judge. Or, to stay in the sphere of images, the God-
image has become a trapeze for subtle religious mental
acrobatics. This unconnectedness with the deep layers
of the soul, however, is due to a general atrophy of man's
power of making and perceiving images. The consequences of rationalism as an intellectual iconoclasm were,
in this respect, more devastating than those of the iconoclasm of the Reformation. In regard to this God-image
Jung's statement rings true: "In a psychically undernour-
ished humanity even God cannot thrive." On the other
hand, the danger of the "countermotion" increases, and
in such a situation numinous images can suddenly break
out of the unconscious into the conscious and inundate
it with strange, terrible, mysterious figures of idols. Since
they are in no way in contact with the "enlightened" consciousness, they are unpurified and use the most primitive
means of attack, especially on those who believe themselves immune from all "superstition."

We have shown in the foregoing some universally
acknowledged backgrounds of the sick God-image. The
problem is in focus even though it could not be laid
open in all its forms, which vary in each individual case.
The significance and the hazards of the God-image demand an ever new examination and control of its procla-

mation, its representation, and its forms as experienced in the innermost personal center. "The thing that cures the neurosis must be as convincing as the neurosis. . . ."[2] Even though in the individual case it remains difficult or impossible to transmit a completely adequate God-image, since "We see now through a mirror in an obscure manner" (1 Cor. 13), it should be possible to avoid great distortions or even a neuroticization. To the Christian, God has become radiant in the countenance of Christ, in the breadth and boundless polarity of the numinous primordial image. Therefore, Paul tells us to "become conformed to the image of his Son" (Rom. 8:29). In the true and unmutilated image of Christ we meet something more convincing than anything a neurosis can provoke: The "glory as of the only begotten of the Father" (John 1:14). Herewith the question of the authentic, integral, and undistorted God-image becomes the no less important question of the Christ-image.

[2] Jung, *Psychology and Religion* (*Collected Works*, Bollingen Series XX [New York: Pantheon] vol. 11, 1958) 105.

CHAPTER IX

Psychotherapy and Spiritual Guidance

It should indeed be a surprise for us to hear psycho-therapy and spiritual guidance spoken of in the same breath. After all, they are clearly distinguished from each other by the specific and diverse goals intrinsic to them, as well as by the diverse ways in which they try to reach their specific goals. If, despite this, we intend to establish a close relationship between the two, the task of this section must be that of showing our reasons for doing so. A good start may be to point out an extrinsic circumstance which allows them to approach each other more closely: the fact of today's growing need of both psychotherapeutic treatment and true spiritual guidance by spiritually and psychologically experienced priests.

It would hardly be correct to assume that the need of psychotherapy has been awakened only because of the significant progress made in this type of treatment. It is rather the ever growing need for psychic help that has demanded this progress and has helped it along. Likewise, the need for spiritual guidance does not stem from the fact that today we have an especially distinguished and secure kind of religious spiritual guidance but from the fact that the spiritual-religious *need* of modern man calls for a more appropriate method of spiritual guidance.

Behind both needs, however, stands our *cultural situation*, which no longer finds solutions through the hitherto available means of human guidance. Here we cannot deal in detail with this cultural situation, although a psychology of today's cultural life is overdue and would give us significant insights into the psychology and psychotherapy of the individual. In this connection I am reminded of the still topic work of Karl Jaspers, *Man in the Modern Age*, which represents an important contribution to this subject. What makes today's situation so complex, so that especially the alert and clairaudient individual suffers from it and cannot come to terms with it, is its transitional character. This character of transition causes interior oppositions: individualism versus collectivism; rationalism versus irrationalism; agnostic nihilism versus a longing for mystic immersion. These oppositions create a great existential insecurity that more and more condenses into an actual existential anxiety.

An individual who lives consciously cannot cope with this frightening situation. His interior is a mirror of the external situation—or is it perhaps that the external situation is a picture of the interior? Psychic fragmentation, torment—in short, neuroticization with all its symptoms of imbalance, irritation, and psychic paralysis—are characteristic of the man of the transitional period. This is why the need for psychotherapeutic treatment and spiritual guidance has grown so much.

In former times it was natural that people took their various spiritual problems to the priest. In most cases he knew what advice to give to help the individual out of his difficulty, or at least could lead him toward a healthy and fruitful endurance of conflicts which could not be changed. Today, however, many people are not even acquainted with their pastor and no longer have, or perhaps can no longer have, confidence in his ability to help them in their psychic needs. Even the religious person feels that much spiritual advice bounces against a blank wall inside him and sets up only hollow reverberations. True, the conflicts are often primarily of a religious nature, but one feels that the psychic situation must first be brought under control by *natural* means. Following religious advice seems dishonest, like a short circuit or an overhasty leap, or mere escape from a reality that could be coped with in a natural and human way. In certain cases, a religious solution may really be searched for and accepted, but the ways and means toward its accomplishment seem no longer adjusted to the new state of the psychic situation, seem somehow too simple. Powers are in play which are *not* addressed by a religious appeal to the intellect and will, powers which at best could be reached only by a *gratia extraordinaria* and which otherwise *autonomously* set up counteractions against all good intentions. Even a relatively healthy individual seeks today for more subtle religious guidance. Finally, there are cases which because of their pathological condition could never be handled by a spiritual director; these appear to be on the increase in our times.

These comments should suffice to explain to some intent the urgency of the "psychotherapy and spiritual guidance" question. Now let us first try to expose the difficulties that make a good relationship between psychotherapy and spiritual guidance problematic. After that we will show how each of them, as a result of its inner development, is approaching the other; finally we shall present a few cases in which the spiritual adviser may or should advise psychotherapeutic treatment.

I DIFFICULTIES BETWEEN PSYCHOTHERAPY AND SPIRITUAL GUIDANCE

The relationship between these two arts of human guidance is at times more apprehensive than friendly. Therefore, it may be proper to start our discussion with the difficulties between them, so that we can then deal more honestly with the possibilities of a fruitful meeting. Let us give the right of precedence to the guides of the spiritual life.

1 The Apprehensions of Spiritual Guidance Regarding Psychotherapy

It is understandable that the much older practice of spiritual guidance voices serious doubts concerning the relatively quite young science of psychotherapy. Disregarding the more unessential difficulties which not infrequently can be traced back to a "hidden resistance" and a fear of the difficult task of analytical treatment or which may be a reaction to the arrogance of a few psychotherapists who fail to respond to the great responsibility demanded in each and every analysis, we find three difficulties worth considering:

a) The much denounced *psychologism* takes first place. Psychologism has various faces. It is still relatively harmless when it suggests that every neurosis must, à *tout prix*, be analyzed away. Quite long ago Igor Caruso wrote vehemently against this extreme analysis-addiction (especially in the form it assumed in the United States). Considering that today less severe forms of neurosis are more frequent and their cause is seldom completely unconscious, it often seems better that the individual learn to honestly put up with his neurosis and by so doing overcome that false perfectionism which, as we know, quite often contributes to neurotic behavior.

It is also psychologism when all manifestations of scientific, artistic, social, political, and religious life are too rashly seen from a psychological slant or simply labeled according to a certain doctrine of neurosis. This psychologism in particular has made enemies for psychology in many fields. Of course, no one with common sense will deny that a science can, hypothetically, look at everything from its specific viewpoint. The fact that for most people the psychic viewpoint carries with it something unpleasant and frightening cannot be avoided and is often only evidence of their inner insecurity. Nevertheless, the psychotherapist, especially because of his psychotherapeutic way of thinking, should strive to overcome the bad habit of psychological monomania and should make the *true* value of his science and art known at the right time, i.e., when one really needs his help. The more the psychotherapist lives as an integral human being, the less he is nothing but psychologist and the more confidence he will instill.

Psychologism becomes most embarrassing when it leads to an almost *systematic dilution* of all metapsychic realities. The reality of the soul is certainly important and fascinating, but physical and metaphysical realities are likewise certain and significant. Perhaps some psychologists are not sufficiently aware that even the process of "projection" often has, as precondition, objective bases that ought to be taken seriously. On the other hand, of course, the accusation of panpsychism should not be rashly made against renowned scientists who, misguided by the nineteenth-century concept of science, so limit their field of research that their precautions not to transgress the boundaries of this realm can almost be interpreted as a rejection of other realms of reality. (This is an accusation which Jung has frequently defended himself against.)

b) The most violent opposition to psychotherapy arises when psychologism becomes a habitual *naturalism*, that is, when all religious actions and forms of piety and all expressions of philosophical thought are declared suspect. Although it is valid to write of a "psychology of ideologies," it is invalid and contradictory to go beyond all empirical facts with one's own psychological interpretations. A milder, more practical naturalism is found in cases where, over an extensive period, prayer and the sacraments are in no way recommended to Catholic patients and the strictly natural psychic development becomes more important and central than a gradual Christian maturation.

c) A further objection often made against psychotherapeutic treatment concerns a phenomenon seen in many who have undergone analysis in the past or those currently undergoing analysis: *loss of spontaneity*. At times these people lose all straightforwardness and frequently, as a consequence, all warmth and sincere cordiality. Everything is experienced in an observing, reflexive way, every mistake in oneself or others is minutely recorded, each possible "compensation" or "substitution" is checked, every dream interpreted and every religious stirring scrutinized as to whether it may perhaps be a remnant of infantilism or a magic, prelogical attitude and evidence of lack of inner substance. All this might be important for the psychotherapist and for the patient *during* the analysis, but, to my mind, after the analysis the patient should once more find his unanalyzed approach to life. Only then can he be truly cured, since, as we know, self-reflexion, as a kind of brooding and self-analysis, is often the very symptom of neurosis.

2 Psychotherapy's Complaints Against Spiritual Guidance

If spiritual advisers want to be heard in their complaints against psychotherapy, then these same advisers should not be sensitive when psychotherapists have certain complaints of their own. Here again we are not speaking about certain prejudices stemming from lack of acquaint-

ance with classical spiritual guidance nor of those prejudices which are clearly a resistance against religious
dogmas and rites. (The latter should especially cause
suspicion to the depth psychologist.) But we would
like to take up three objections that seem to have some
justification.

a) *Supranaturalism* is the first complaint, and this can
hardly surprise us. Time and again practicing psychotherapists have the impression that some spiritual advisers
have not the slightest understanding of natural values
and powers and of the God-given instincts of man. Such
spiritual advisers, from one point of view, naïvely encourage all kinds of repressions and see many forms of psychic blocking and even paralysis and emotional atrophy
as signs of progress. At the same time, from another point
of view they support the need for a magical and mystical
satisfaction and thus cultivate unhealthy and dangerous
psychic attitudes. We might mention here how much
hysterical phenomena, such as visions, hearing voices,
and so forth, are on the increase today.[1]

b) The second complaint against spiritual advisers may
hurt even more; it is that of *legalism*, of a mere legalistic
piety. Psychotherapists have had their fill of pious people
who keep commandments only out of fear or out of a
letter-of-the-law attitude. Such people seek to be absolved
from their guilt without discovering the symbolic content

---

[1] There have been innumerable "apparitions of our Lady" during the
last twenty years in the most diverse places. For the facts, cf. *Orientie-
rung*, 1951, no. 23–24. The mass hysteria of Heroldsbach is also probably a symptom of misguided piety.

of its symptoms, without asking themselves why they compulsively and constantly lie or why they habitually reduce their fellowman to a thing, the object of their own need of assertion. These individuals have no realization that a certain attitude toward "chastity" is frequently only a fear of sexuality as such and of the responsibility connected with it; for many this is a great cause of repressions rather than the control of a truly powerful, mature sexuality in the sense of a freely willed choice of life.

Closely connected with legalism is a *compulsive factor* which reveals the inner unfreedom of these individuals. It is as though the observance of commandments and prohibitions is bound up to the idea of a magic safety belt of life. Certain regulations so completely take on the character of the taboo that the person's vital development is strangled and he can no longer speak of an authentic morality. He avoids what the book tells him is evil (is this an *actus humanus?*) and offers up all his difficulties as "trials" sent him from God, without questioning in what sense something is a trial, *why* it hurts, and how deeply it affects him. Difficulties dealt with in this way cannot be productive for man. Or again, a person may pray ten times a day for his enemies: "Father forgive him for he knows not what he does," but he does not investigate the cause and meaning of this hostility. Certain terms are also often magically misused: purity, poverty, obedience—all great ideals which in individual cases can degenerate into mere schemata. Meekness and gentleness can certainly be the result of long and painful striving, but at times they can also be cowardice, passivity, and fear of contradiction: One is still the frightened boy, insecure and intimidated by all authority—completely unaware of a father complex. Often this reproach of legalism is not taken seriously enough. Many don't really believe that even the faithful (and the faithful, above all), going beyond a state of heteronomous piety and practice of virtue, want to and must answer questions which arise out of their personal conscience and in the face of conflicts of conscience created by our differentiated culture. Yet any psychotherapist can assure us that even the seemingly simple people feel the heavy weight of these problems today. Some of them eventually go ahead on their own and find a solution according to their own conscience and feeling without paying much attention to hitherto licit rules, while others, after a few attempts to get priestly understanding, finally go to a psychotherapist. It seems that this entire problematic complex should be more honestly recognized and more broad-mindedly attended to in Christian confidence. Of course there cannot be so much as a start toward solution without a corresponding training of the clergy.

c) A third reproach is more understandable and with even the best intention of spiritual advisers cannot be completely eliminated: Spiritual guidance is often accused of being merely a *treatment of symptoms*. Since, as we know, spiritual guidance deals with the conscious experiences of man, with the more or less clearly recognized sins and virtues, it does not penetrate into the unconscious undergrounds of these acts, into their psychic interconnections and strange disguises. This means that the spiritual adviser often does not reach into and deal with the actual causes of a failure and the true motives of virtuous acts. In the light of depth psychology's insights, certain ascetical axioms seem not only ineffective but even directly dangerous for psychic health, especially for the authenticity of religious life—for instance, for imprudent, radical axiom "*agere contra.*" In less complex times radical means may have been sometimes helpful, but today they can effect the contrary of what is hoped for. Whoever focuses *exclusively* on symptoms, without being able to see them in context and penetrate into their backgrounds, may cause in healthy persons years of stagnation in their religious life, a psychic sterility which can even become a psychic paralysis. In the less healthy persons such ascesis works like an enormous apparatus of repression with all its momentous consequences.

It should be clear, then, how difficult satisfactory spiritual guidance is and always will be. After all, one cannot expect that every part-time and even full-time spiritual adviser has both theoretical and practical knowledge of all these complicated questions. One thing we must emphasize, and that is that priests and spiritual directors should not practice psychotherapy. The consequences could be even more disastrous than anything mentioned in our discussion.

II THE RAPPROCHEMENT OF PSYCHOTHERAPY AND SPIRITUAL GUIDANCE

If the relationship of psychotherapy and spiritual guidance were completely aired in a discussion of their mutual concerns and difficulties, one would be tempted to speak of two hostile brothers. Fortunately, we observe what appears to be a promising development, so much so that we believe we can rightly speak of a friendly meeting, perhaps even of a rapprochement and possibility of collaboration. It will be of value to reflect for a moment on the development of both of these forms of human guidance.

1 The Development of Psychotherapy[2]

It seems almost superfluous to backtrack over the long and yet so fast-traveled road of psychotherapy, from Freud and Adler to Jung, then to the fate-analysis of Szondi, and from Frankl's logotherapy up to the personalistic analysis of Caruso.[3] I believe I can speak of a development, because, while on the one hand essential positions and statements have remained the same, on the other hand progress at one point is unmistakably observable.

Four points have been consistently agreed upon:
a) In respect to the *manifestation* of neurosis: Diverse though this be, it is nevertheless always clearly characterized by a habitual lack of adjustment, by the well-known

[2] We take for granted that the difference between psychiatry and any form of psychotherapy is acknowledged at least theoretically and generally also in practice. Psychiatry reserves for itself all so-called psychoses, that is, all cases of manifest or latent mental illness, epilepsies, manic-depressive psychosis, and all forms of schizophrenia, whether purely hereditary or perhaps reactive in their origin, while psychotherapy attempts to treat the multifarious forms of neurosis.

[3] We make no mention here of the existenzanalyse of L. Binswanger and the daseinsanalyse of M. Boss, since they are philosophical tendencies and thus differ in principle from those dealt with here.

disproportion in external behavior or interior states: psychic explosivity, conditions of long-lasting excitation, or, conversely, deep depressions even to the point of paralysis. Equally well-known are the organic symptoms such as heart and stomach neurosis, and so forth. In these, a more or less intensive compulsive factor always plays a role, so that the lack of adjustment takes place as though "autonomously" in its symptoms.

b) In respect to the *basis* of neurosis: There is agreement as to the fact that very often *unconscious* conflicts stay in the background and, therefore, the treatment demands an investigation of the unconscious realm. Hereby we always find a certain *lawfulness* regarding psychic energy and its focal points, the complexes. The laws of constancy and equivalence, the law of the regulating function of the opposites (as a kind of psychic entropy), the law of a certain teleology (as the law of an impending developmental phase) are well-known. We may also point out the law of projection with its significance for interhuman relationships and the law of "enantiodromia": the psychic opposition of tendencies and countertendencies. We deal here with laws in the broadest sense. Whoever has psychotherapeutic contact with people can observe that the actuality of these laws and of their disconcerting functioning is constantly newly confirmed.

But this unconscious with its lawfulness belongs to the *nature* of man. It participates actively in all his behavior, be it as a mere material or as an energetic complex, and it participates all the more intensively, the less he knows or wants to know about its lawfulness. This unconscious *is part of* human nature which, as we know, is not only spirit but also matter made living. Therefore, the realm of the unconscious must be taken into proper consideration. Its influence is much greater than one is generally willing to accept. Through scientific-empirical investigation the nature of man stands more clearly before us and is more clearly recognized. Every act of man receives a depth from the many-layered nature of man and, consequently, is often enough open to various interpretations. For the question will always arise as to which is the actual "layer" that is springboard for the act.

c) A third feature common to all these approaches is the use of *analysis* as a systematic method for investigating the unconscious. Whether one uses the classical analytical procedure of Sigmund Freud and his school or applies analysis more as a cooperative working out of the unconscious depths in Jung's way, perhaps even consciously stressing personal conversation (in the sense of Hans Trüb, etc.)—it is, in any case, a matter of the very methodical *activation* of the psychic powers in order to attain a greater person-integration. Dreams, active imagination, free painting and drawing, musical improvisation and composition are expressions of the soul providing the expert with information concerning the unconscious, the relative health or sickness of the psychic life, and consequently also the contents that need to be assimilated.

d) The fourth common feature is the proximate goal of psychotherapy. It demands that man regain the *free disposal* of his psychic energy and so become newly adjusted to reality. Beyond this proximate goal are other goals closely connected with the deeper *interpretation* of neurosis. Here, however, the differences begin, and agreement among the various approaches has not yet been reached, even though there appears to be a strong mutual influence.

e) There is a difference in the *interpretation:* For Freud's followers neurosis remains essentially a product of *repression.* Experiences of early childhood, above all those which in the broadest sense belong to the sexual sphere, have been repressed into the personal-unconscious as if into a wastebasket. They lead to a complex-formation that sooner or later produces neurotic symptoms.

Jung's school goes beyond this to maintain that neurosis is a deficiency of psychic development, not only of some dispositions but even of structure-given psychic qualities and images of the collective unconscious,[4] which, over and above all individual experience, is common to man as man. The so-called "shadow" and the psychic images of "anima" and "animus" are not so much repressed but have for the most part remained in their primitive state and therefore exercise a neurotic effect of interpersonal relationships. Also, what Jung calls the "archetypes" requires an honest examination. Above all, however, Jung himself emphasizes that on the ground of every human soul the natural God-image, the archetype of God, lies dormant and that from the middle of

---

[4] The concept of the collective-unconscious was originally explained by Jung phylogenetically, based on the idea of development. Later on Jung left open the genesis of these unconscious contents. Yet their description corresponds to a great degree to that which the philosophy of being calls the psychic "structure."

life on it should no longer be ignored. "Among all my patients in the second half of life—that is to say, over thirty-five—there has not been one whose problem in the last resort was not that of finding a religious outlook on life. It is safe to say that every one of them fell ill because he had lost that which the living religions of every age have given to their followers, and none of them has been really healed who did not regain his religious outlook."[5]

Thus, neurosis is here no longer merely a product of repression but one of underdevelopment in general, of an underdevelopment of the authentic image of man and its deepest developmental tendency.

A further step now leads us to the conception that neurosis is in its meaning the result of an *absolutizing* of merely relative values, as Caruso has convincingly explained. Many fixations and regressions, as well as the substitutions and identifications time and again observed in religious life, point to such false absolutizing. Without making Freud's and Jung's hypotheses superfluous, this reveals a main root of all neurosis formation, which, perhaps, has always been known in religious circles but which was not proved with the exactitude of a scientific-empirical method.

Finally, we should not bypass Viktor Frankl's logotherapy, since this is the approach which most encompasses the spiritual dimensions of man and proves that

[5] Jung, *Modern Man in Search of a Soul* (New York: Harcourt, Brace, 1933) 229.

a false resolution or the repression of spiritual problems may be formative of neurosis.

When we consider these different interpretations of neurosis, the question arises whether the views of the various schools do actually clash or whether they complement one another. This may even be proof of a developmental process, of a development whose foundations were possibly already laid in the beginnings of psychotherapy. Consequently, it has become increasingly clear that it is a matter of man, of his natural wholeness and completeness, of his psychic and physical health, of his interior development, even of the God-image which the Creator has given him when he created him according to his image and parable. This man is supposed to take over the full responsibility of his life and his actions. Man is no longer to live in ignorance of the abysses of his own soul but to strive to live with clear insight into the complex layers and undergrounds, superstructures and laws of his nature. Through his very neurosis he has been awakened to be no longer the semiconscious plaything of the events of his nature but to take on mature and conscious responsibility for them.

Even though the development of psychotherapy has by no means reached a final solution of the problem of methods and specific goals, one can see that new and very essential positions have been gained in the understanding of neurosis, and these must be discussed. At the same time psychotherapy has hereby come closer to what was formerly considered the task of spiritual guidance.

2   *Spiritual Guidance*

Spiritual guidance, despite the contrary impression, has seldom been content with mere direction of conscience. Anyone who went beyond the ordinary concept of pastoral care as proclamation and confessional advice and followed the truly great schools of spiritual guidance was aware of the fact that spiritual guidance is ultimately a question of the formation of the *entire* life. Great spiritual advisers, too, sensed that there was something in back of the striving for perfection. They knew the manifold dangers of religious striving, knew something of what today we call displacement, masking, substitution, and identification, and even unconscious egotistical motivations were no secret to them. Of course, it was usually the more intuitively gifted spiritual advisers who possessed these insights and put them into practice, since it took hundreds of years for even the skimpiest beginnings of a scientifically systematic method. It was especially these centuries-old experiences that gave the religious orders their solid traditions, which, in general, have continually proved their worth. In short, even classical spiritual guidance meant to consider the whole man. Today, however, the leaders of religious life sense all the more clearly the necessity of a true insight into psychic foundations and laws, for those to be guided are, after all, people of a very complex cultural situation. Thus, we might say that psychotherapy, interpreted in the broadest sense, and spiritual guidance are approaching each other ever more closely and that a fruitful meeting between them is possible and desirable. But in order to realize this encounter it is indispensable to point up and work out more precisely the specific difference of each one's influence on man, so that we may see more clearly what they have in common. In plain words, the question is: To what extent do psychotherapy and spiritual guidance differ in regard to their aim and their methods?

a) First, it can certainly be said that for psychotherapy the most comprehensive goal is the complete man as realization of the natural God-image, while the goal of spiritual guidance consists in the perfect man in the sense of supernatural holiness. Completion is not perfection.

Though the difference is clear, it will be difficult to keep to it in practice. Is not some Catholic spiritual guidance unconsciously rooted in the theology of the Reformation and, as a result, does it not try to approach man solely from the side of revelation, without considering natural dispositions? But a truly Catholic spiritual guidance can never separate nature and supernature. Since the order of salvation in no way cancels out the order of creation and since grace is generally based on nature and elevates it, the entire realm of this nature necessarily becomes important and topical even for spiritual guidance. The final supernatural goal must be endeavored for in partial goals, which in turn must take the psychic developmental phases into consideration. Regardless of whether one bases the striving for perfection more on grace or more on the personal effort of the will, it will always be a matter of total life-formation.

Therefore the problem "health and holiness" is by no

means a pseudoproblem. God can certainly make use of neurosis and has probably often done so in order to lead a person toward holiness. However, at that point where the striving for perfection attains a certain continuity and an inner, long-lasting authenticity, psychic health must also improve in the form of personal integration and adjustment to reality, even though some external neurotic symptoms may be never completely vanquished. (As we know, psychotherapy, too, is not a complete cure but only tries to put man on a psychic track that gradually leads to healthier regions.) Of course, certain symptoms —for example pseudologia phantastica, states of uncontrolled excitement, or long-lasting depressions—seem to us incompatible with true perfection. Thus, as soon as the goal of spiritual guidance is no longer seen merely theoretically, it becomes evident that the psychotherapeutic goal of psychic integration and completion should often be included as part of the goal of spiritual guidance.

b) Will the difference between psychotherapy and spiritual guidance appear essentially greater once we have reflected on the means used by each? Here again, certainly the basic difference must be emphasized: Spiritual guidance works with grace, prayer, meditation, the sacraments, and with the cooperation of the faithful in using these means. From the very beginning these are and remain completely different from the means used by psychotherapy. However, in the application of these remedies, the psychological viewpoint cannot completely be ignored. The psychic tides must be under constant surveillance. These remedies should be administered in prudent doses, for otherwise they may become detrimental —"*cotidiana vilescunt*"—or, at any rate, fail to produce any favorable effects. All too often one gets the impression that some spiritual guides use favorite "cookbook" remedies which result in developmental misdirections entirely to be expected.

An actual encounter between depth psychology and spiritual guidance in regard to means should take place when we come to the question of *ascesis*. Ascesis is, after all, a "natural" means which we find in many religions and which therefore is particularly in danger of being passed on too matter-of-factly and without examination. Ascesis as the mortification of natural instincts and renunciation of the fulfillment of natural desire can become one-sided, especially when it is not deepened through the law of the cross and active obedience. Then, in "mortifying his nature" one forgets that this nature is not a thin surface but has many layers. Not infrequently, in that case, the law of "mutual opposition" of the instincts comes into play. When, for instance, the sexual instincts are merely repressed instead of being worked out, a very intolerant, even aggressive drive of assertion may start on a rampage and often becomes further camouflaged by religious motives. Or one renounces a development that would require courage and responsibility and surrenders passively to a submissiveness which seems to be conscientiousness and obedience, while in reality it not only strangles all psychic development but also gradually paralyzes external initiative. And more follows: One stops short with his so-called "good conscience" in apparent full agreement with the objective moral code, but as a result of this there are the most uncouth repressions of sex and even repression of the need of experiencing deeper values. Therefore, the individual remains fixated upon a phase of childhood, which by no means should be confused with Christ's command that we become as children. The highly esteemed happiness of the cloister is not always a treasure and a sign of the God-willed way of life; sometimes it is merely a sign of stagnated development and passive immaturity.

And so spiritual guidance cannot give standard prescriptions but must be flexible. In practice this means: At every phase of life the problems of the affective, instinctual, and religious life must be newly solved on an objective basis, for the forty-year-old is no longer twenty; if he were, it would signify that an inner psychic development failed to occur. This intrapsychic stagnation, whether it is due to excessive external activism or to less reputable reasons, will sooner or later result in conflicts that will affect family and professional life.

We should also say a word about the *collective ascesis* considered valid for all members of a community without distinction. This ascesis is, of course, necessary in some respects, but it is also often wasteful and sometimes even directly detrimental. Today's cultural situation, with its pronounced individualism and complicatedness (qualities that show up most among the "elite"), demands an ascesis that takes each one's psychic individuality into consideration with a delicate sensitivity for nuances. Otherwise years of mechanized ascetical exercises may never reach the decisive point of person formation. Instead of a concretely living ascesis, we find an abstract and exclusive one, stemming not from freedom but from legalism. Here again the cross is raised without the least awareness that at this particular moment there is no man to be nailed upon it but only an unfree person still stuck in infantilism.

Thus depth psychology and spiritual guidance can meet each other even regarding the matter of means, and a closer approximation is desirable.

III   WHEN SHOULD THE SPIRITUAL ADVISER RECOMMEND PSYCHOTHERAPEUTIC TREATMENT?

The following deliberations will be of a practical nature, although I am well aware that they will raise new questions of theory, for instance, in respect to the principles leading to collaboration between spiritual adviser and psychotherapist. Yet it seems premature to deal at this time with questions which must be the fruit of many individual experiences. Another aspect should be mentioned: In all our previous considerations we have referred to neurotic symptoms, but in the concrete individual case the question of the ever present somatic and psychotic components must immediately be investigated. This means that in certain cases the physician and the psychiatrist must also be consulted, since neurosis not infrequently represents only a superimposition on already existent pathological processes. In these cases psychotherapeutic treatment could be very dangerous and in some instances lead to the activation of a dormant psychosis.

In this connection we should again recall that it is neither necessary nor advisable to subject every neurosis to analytical treatment. In some cases even neurotic illness can become the test that gives rise to the patience by which an individual possesses his soul. Also the great expenditure of time and money demanded by a complete analysis should limit it to cases in which a meaningful formation of life and the fulfillment of professional or family obligations is at stake. In what follows we shall briefly allude to such cases, without of course making any claim to completeness.

Analysis seems to be necessary in many cases of *sexual perversion*, which, as we know, is often caused by repression or fixation. Homosexuality, excessive masturbation, Don Juanism, nymphomania are sometimes indicative of an infantile phase of psychic development or an escape from personal responsibility. Yet only a trained analyst can help here. In fact, these perversions have such disturbing and destructive effects on human life that analytic treatment is imperative whenever the financial situation allows it. Authentic religious life particularly is poisoned by such aberrations, since, even in cases of compulsive sexuality, guilt feelings generally come to the fore and time and again drive the compulsive neurotic to look for new compensations.

Certain cases of intense, inexplicable *guilt feelings* should also be directed to an analyst. It is the perpetual characteristic of many neuroses that they are accompanied by such guilt feelings. There are no sins to be recognized as such, and even imperfections would be very welcome to provide an explanation for the guilt feeling. Such constant guilt feelings, however, can turn into heavy feelings of inferiority and rob the person entirely of his initiative and joy in work. Such people walk under a dark cloud, always somehow low-spirited, perhaps merely with a subaltern attitude, even though their capacities could accommodate much greater aspirations. It takes a very thorough analysis to unravel the cause of such guilt feelings. It may be that repressions occurred with the greatest matter-of-factness. But an excessive perfectionism also often leads to a guilt complex. One wishes to achieve a fullness of virtue for which God has not yet given the necessary grace. One seeks to be the angel but must always realize that he is but a human being of flesh and blood.

Behind such angelism and perfectionism we should not unconditionally look for only great virtuous striving and high idealism. Such an attitude is often the hiding place for unadmitted drives of self-assertion, for compulsive ideas, primitive taboos, or camouflaged egotistical desires, even though they may have a religious character. It can also be a matter of an "octroi" from without, when the environment systematically and yet thoughtlessly cultivates overheated emotions or even gives them expression in the form of prayers, feelings which can hardly ever or may never be truly achieved over a long period of time.

Neurosis should also be treated by a specialist whenever it is a typical *expression of a life-lie*, of a completely unconscious year-after-year untruthfulness with oneself.

Should this untruthfulness become a permanent resistance or, indeed, a rebellion against his intrinsic life-order
and life-task, the neurotic finds himself in the infamous
"diabolical circle" in which overcompensations and guilt
feelings grow ever more intensive and push him into a
situation of inner hopelessness. Then the life-lie causes
that deep existential unrest and anxiety which no medical
or religious palliative can alleviate. Igor Caruso coined
the term "life-heresy" for this situation and thus exposed
the false centering of the neurotic. It would be a mistake
to think that "life-heresies" are found only in those outside of the Church or principally in the laity; they are
probably just as typical for religious persons, since it is
not easy to approach the absolute always from the same
direction.

The question of whether the spiritual director should
recommend analysis becomes extremely complicated
when an individual seems as if possessed by an almost
self-destructive *longing to suffer.* There are seemingly
very pious people who forever feel the urge to sacrifice
themselves for others or to renounce everything good,
beautiful, and pleasant. Every joy they would like to
permit themselves is suspect and as a rule finally refused.
They seek everywhere only the cross and its suffering.
Everywhere? Really? Even though they perhaps radiate
a calm cheerfulness and may be quiet and taciturn, they
can be inwardly tormented, restless, and fragmented,
passionately yearning for that compensation which out-
weighs all their renunciations: the *religious satisfaction*
of their delight in suffering. There is—and many do not

wish to admit it—a masochistic component in play which finds its very satisfaction in being the most unworthy, the very last, the most simple, the most useless servant of all the servants of God. (Generally, however, they are maidservants!) The desire to develop oneself, to form and unfold one's own personality is then branded as pride and sin—and finally one can no longer accept his own existence without guilt feelings. What should the spiritual adviser do in such a case? Perhaps some telling symptoms are still in evidence: Strange symptoms of paralysis, long dragged-out convalescences after almost insignificant illnesses indicate a secret addiction to the benefits in all these sufferings. Such persons often make the priest the confidant of their suffering addiction so that he will confirm their being on the right way. This frees them from their own responsibility and allows them to yield to their disguised needs with an easier conscience. There may also be many years of stagnation of the life of grace, indicating that underground something pathological is going on even though there seems to be no visible and expressible guilt.

Analysis will probably be necessary for a person who suffers from *demonomania* and may believe himself possessed by the devil or who has visual, auditory, or tactile hallucinations of demons. But, especially in these cases, what is first required is medical and psychiatric examination if psychotherapy is to be effectual without the danger of activating a full-blown mental illness. Although in the lives of some saints actual powers of evil have been experienced, in most of the cases we meet we should remember the axiom: *"Daemonia supponit naturam,"* which means that demonomania presupposes a nature suffering from some kind of abnormal symptoms, be it only a state of pathological fear. By this we imply that in very rare cases exorcism may be in order, but generally the need is for a psychotherapist.

Finally, it must be assumed that most cases of religious scrupulosity will require psychotherapeutic treatment if years of failure and misdirections are to be avoided.

In conclusion, let us ask once more if it would not be of greater advantage to emphasize the mutual approach and friendly collaboration of psychotherapy and spiritual guidance rather than the difficulties between them. This would cause neither psychotherapy nor spiritual guidance to lose its proper nature and independence. Spiritual guidance must remain within the conscious realm. True, it is good for spiritual guidance to be well versed in the unconscious psychic life, to keep it always in view, and to act cautiously in its regard. But psychotherapy's task is to descend into the unconsciousness when it is necessary. On the other hand, psychotherapy can certainly profit from a constant awareness that even in the compulsive neurotic there is a conscious realm of the soul, and, at least indirectly, the will power of these patients should be strengthened. Thus psychotherapy can never become a mere servant of spiritual guidance as long as it is a servant of the whole person, and spiritual guidance will not turn into a mere prophylaxis of neurosis if it keeps in mind that neurosis also interferes with religious life and at times makes it impossible. Both

should help man to form his life integrally and meaningfully and to lead it beyond relativities toward an absolute.

It seems to us that our present cultural situation often
demands a collaboration of psychotherapy and spiritual
guidance, but we hope for a time when man once again
can more easily live a wholesome and integral life.

CHAPTER X

Neurosis—Perfectionism—Piety

The recognition and emphasis of the positive aspects in the neurotic process represents an essential progress in the study of neuroses. True, it is still important to point out repeatedly that neurosis is a symptom of repression, of denial, of psychic undevelopment, and of a compensation mechanism. But it is equally important never to forget that neurosis is also always an attempt of the soul to make up for an at least halfway sensed weakness, to master a life-situation, and to meet a deeply hidden, nagging conflict. Paradoxical though it seems, even neurosis is in the service of life, of life-affirmation. Consciously or unconsciously, the neurotic seeks a way out of a psychic dead-end street. In his very depths be believes in an answer to his seemingly insoluble problem, and he tries desperately to find a way of freedom leading out of the narrow pass into which he—with or without guilt—has worked himself. Only one who views this exhausting, strength-sapping struggle of the neurotic in a positive and understanding way and with the same attitude makes his first evaluations of it can hope to find access to the soul of the neurotic and to the deeply buried roots of his misery.

Neurosis by itself fails to give a satisfactory answer to the problem of the neurotic individual. It does not help him out of his conflict but, on the contrary, drives him into a *circulus vitiosus*, into a diabolical circle of instinct denial and ersatz satisfactions which shrinks more and more into a narrow, stifling prison. He may beat his head on the walls in despair or fall down as though paralyzed; there seems to be no door out of this ever more constricting prison. It is the tragedy of the neurotic individual that often enough he has the "best intentions" of pulling down the walls of his prison and breaking through the suit of armor encasing him, but instead he makes the walls stronger and higher and the suit of armor tighter and tighter. Every therapist knows from the dreams of his patients how apt is this image of the prison and the suit of armor. How can a man free himself if he is locked in a narrow, fifteen-foot-high concrete cylinder with no ladder nor even chinks in the wall? Such was the dream of a highly educated professor who was at the point of suffocation in his marriage while suffering from his own guilt feelings to such a degree that in his relationship with his wife he could display only an insecure and weak attitude which directly provoked her aggression. Even though neurosis may evidence a hidden "good intention" and an effort to solve a life-problem, and even though this exceptionally good intention should be positively evaluated and this ever-so-honest effort acknowledged, not for a single moment should it be forgotten how improper and hopeless, even dangerous and destructive is this entire behavior of the neurotic and how completely wrong and unauthentic is his answer to the question so inexorably posed to him by life.

Why is it not possible for the neurotic to find the right attitude, to form his life in a more healthy and humanly free manner? Why does it reach the point that such a person finally has an anxiety dream in which he sees himself locked behind iron bars while pitch unremittingly drips from above so that he is enveloped by this hot mess and becomes gradually immobilized?

At first glance there seem to be several answers to this question; this is why several theories of neurosis have been established and yet so one-sidedly that Jung deliberately chose to ignore such theories. The more one reflects on the various answers and lets the tone of their expression be fully heard, the more he can perceive the one answer resonating behind them all: The neurotic individual suffers from *reality*. He bangs his head against its walls, and his hands are sore from rattling the bars. For, basically, he is not ready to accept the hardships or the limitations and inadequacies of reality. He has a set idea of the world, of men and things which becomes his only valid and indisputable dominant image for what absolutely must be and what alone is allowed to be. Reality must bend to his idea, must adjust; otherwise it is ignored, refused, and condemned. The neurotic individual also has a very definite idea of how his therapist should be and tries to force even him to behave in accordance with this image. He is a perfectionist. This is his secret, his seeming happiness, and his never ending suffering. Perfectionism is his unrecognized (because inhibited) greatness, his "virtue," and his power, and it brings his unstable dynamics into action; but it is also his psychic cancer which over and over causes him to become blocked and paralyzed by disappointments and bitterness or to break out into terrible storms of rebellion and accusation. What is there about this perfectionism?

NEUROSIS AS PERFECTIONISM

Whoever is unfamiliar with psychotherapy does not comprehend the statement that all neurotics are perfectionists; yet for the therapist this is a well-known fact. We hear again and again expressions like: "One must do the perfect," "it is a matter of absolute justice," "one need only want to and one can." A twenty-year-old girl with a masklike rigidity once told me very matter-of-factly: "All the others can have their weaknesses, but I cannot have them and do not want to have them." Was she a young saint? Not long before she had committed an objectively serious offense against the moral law and consequently suffered a psychic breakdown. Now her image of a saint was forever shattered and its pieces scattered in the dust. Subjectively, however, she became the victim of her own compulsive mechanisms which she had provoked by her exaggerated perfectionist complex in accordance with the law of mutual opposition. It is the curse of the perfectionistic will that its rigidity and stubbornness activates the antagonism of the repressed instincts within the unconscious and generally causes them to break through.

Let us try to bring the separate elements of perfectionism into sharper focus. It is not enough to simply state that the perfectionist runs against reality and hurts himself because he harbors an idea-image incompatible with reality. We must more precisely delimit those realities that commonly become stumbling blocks for the neurotic and mark off more clearly his concrete idea-image from those inner images which dwell in and also motivate the artist, scientist, politician, and saint.

The mere assertion that the perfectionist is at war with reality could become a cheap slogan opening the way to off-the-cuff standard prescriptions. The solution would be very clear: Tell the perfectionist to put up with reality, to adjust to it and give up his "ideas." Yet this is the very thing the perfectionist is unable to do. It would be just as futile to give him a profound philosophical explanation that this very attitude of not being adjusted to reality is the actual essence of neurosis. This in no way contributes to the improvement or the treatment of the neurotic person.

There is, of course, not a single area of reality which could not become the field of a neurotic process, but certain areas seem to be especially favored. With few exceptions the perfectionist time and again ignores or violently rejects these particular areas of reality and cannot find a productive attitude toward them. It should be clearly understood that a happening that eats itself so deeply into the psychic life as does the severe neurotic process also has corresponding and deep-seated backgrounds which interfere with the nature of man. Offhand one might quickly enumerate some "causes" of neurotic behavior. Yet we know from experience that those realities which have been neglected or are "proudly" and stubbornly refused are generally part of the natural structure of man and cannot simply be thrown into the pile of factual data since they absolutely demand consideration. We shall speak here only about three of these realities which are often ignored.

Frequently the perfectionist cannot find the right *relationship to his body* and his instinct-structure. Although the claim that the Church is hostile to the body is a naïve generalization, unfounded both as official doctrine of the Church and as theological opinion, we must admit that it was not only in earlier times that a seemingly "Christian" hostility of the spirit against the body prevailed. Even today some ascetics restrict themselves to a negative view of the body and seek to reduce its needs to a minimum. The denial of bodily recreation as well as necessary sleep, the disregard of a proper diet both as to quality and quantity are supposed to bring the "insubordinate" body into subjection. Recurrently we run across the conception that a person can proceed almost arbitrarily in these matters, shrugging off the individual constitution, can make decisions of will without regard for the natural rhythm of the body in its need of food, rest, and exercise. An ordering of the instincts which is based upon adequate knowledge of the laws of the instincts, or which is even seen as a sublimation of the instincts, is hardly ever mentioned. The instincts are permitted to be pushed down and arbitrarily dammed up so that they sink with their satisfaction to the level of a primitive animalistic need. Today, of course, this leveling process may not be only religiously and spiritually motivated but is also frequently found among executive types, who in their money-making fervor and work hysteria castigate their body with an unnatural way of living much more than did the ascetics of the Middle Ages.

In the area of the sexual instinct we find similar disorientation and negligence. There are those who are unscrupulously living out their sex pleasure to the full, and there are those—not so many—who try to find a balanced sexual life within the nature-given order, and then there are perfectionists to whom sexuality as such is suspect. The perfectionist is ashamed of this drive as though it would lower man, and he regards his stirrings as "temptations" that must be courageously quelled. The expected consequence is an unbearable damming up of sexual energy. Then, as a rule, this unacknowledged instinct takes its revenge on the psyche: Temptations grow constantly stronger, all devils seem to be literally let loose, and an overheated phantasy projects these demons as hallucinations onto the world around or encounters them in voices and "visions." When even today we repeatedly encounter such situations, we cannot but think that they are the result of serious misinterpretations. Can we not see that behind this instinctual behavior is a clearly Manichean spirituality and that many ascetic practices are not according to the spirit and doctrine of Christianity but have crept in from the world-rejecting attitude of Eastern religions? The realistic and wholesome way of thinking of Thomas Aquinas on this matter often appears to be entirely unknown.[1]

But the pathological phenomenon of hallucinatory voices and visions is not restricted to religiously oriented groups. The increase in these manifestations of psychic split must turn our attention to the cultural situation of today, which cannot be viewed simply as an epoch of a rational and technological attitude which is isolated from the rest of the psychic life (the perfection of technology!). It must also be seen as an epoch of a sexus that has become intensified to the same degree and has developed its own autonomous behavior. The ground swells of both technological reason and of sexus have built up a violent momentum, and yet they go in opposite directions and thus divide the soul into two almost completely separate halves that communicate only in the underground, in accordance with the well-known axiom: *les extrêmes se touchend.* Compulsive ideas, depressions, scruples, and neuroses are an almost automatic and necessary consequence of this disdain of nature's integrity.

Another area of reality which often attracts and fascinates the perfectionist and from which he cannot free himself is *guilt*; yet he never really interiorly resolves it and never wants to admit it. Guilt here is not the juridical or strict moral-theology guilt—which, as we know, presupposes clear insight and a free choice—but rather

[1] Cf. Josef Pieper's valuable study "Temperance" in his *The Four Cardinal Virtues* (Notre Dame, Ind.: University of Notre Dame Press, 1966) 145–206.

the guilt complex of the perfectionist which becomes activated when even the shadow of guilt appears, when it is simply a matter of human weakness and failure and everyday inadequacies. Everywhere and at every instant looms the possibility of becoming guilty, of falling into the mud of life and staining the seemingly snow-white garment. The perfectionist is in constant fear of becoming enmeshed in guilt; in fact, he is convinced that he is already guilty. A murder has been committed. The perfectionist is strangely moved and fascinated by it. He soon "discovers" everywhere the murderer whose picture is in the paper. He feels obliged to search for and to find this monster wherever he goes and to repeatedly call the police in order to keep them informed of his "leads."

Why does this murder so move and fascinate him? Let us take another case: "Did I unplug the iron? It might cause a fire that could burn up the whole house and kill the children! Better call a taxi and rush immediately back to check the iron." What is behind this exaggerated fear of fire? There are thousands of such guilt anxieties. "Can I really accept the Church's permission to eat meat on Friday?" "Was that a 'C' movie I saw?" "Was my smile a come-on to that married man?" "Did I really say my prayers without distraction? I better start them all over again, just to be sure . . . and now, just once again so that I can be at peace." These tormented individuals find no rest by day or night since they wish to do everything absolutely perfectly and unfortunately can never succeed. Doubts by the dozen surround the perfectionist.

Now let us look at the seamy side: If we should tell the perfectionist that he is an egotist thinking only of his immaculate escutcheon (of course we do not tell him this), he would be deeply hurt, begin to tremble, and want to grab us by the throat. Or else he might be immobilized by a dead faint reflex. To accuse oneself is one thing, but to be accused is another. To have to admit one's mistakes because they are pointed out by others, to have to admit that one is not inspired by only the highest motives but has also been seeking his own advantage in spending years on a noble project—this is hard to take! When this happens the perfectionist feels seriously offended; it is a terrible humiliation, almost destroying him. After all, he went through such efforts to be completely perfect and without guilt. Everything in him fights against the acceptance of real guilt, no matter how much imagined guilt he has borne for years. Hasn't he suffered enough already from his unfounded guilt feelings without someone making him responsible for his perhaps well-founded ones? A mild reprimand—not to speak of a severe reproach—brings him to the verge of a crisis. Then "something cracks up inside" him; he "would never have expected this"; "it is unfair," is "dirty and mean." These are strange reactions for a realistic individual who knows about his weaknesses, both great and small, and honestly admits them. But this kind of perfectionism is a disease and turns man into a tormented, miserable being, suffocated by his guilt feelings.

A third realm of reality which often seduces one into perfectionism is justice in its many forms. The idea of an absolute justice terrorizes some persons. What kind of man will the eight-year-old boy become who says to his mother about his little sister: "You've got to punish her 'cause she did wrong"? Will he not develop a fanatical justice which will keep tormenting himself and others until they fulfill the letter of the law? He may develop a need of cleanliness that leads to compulsive hand washing; perhaps a repetition-compulsion, which must always make sure that certain formalities are observed; or a scrupulosity concerning confession, since he cannot be entirely certain that he has true purpose of amendment or that his intention was actually honest. Seen objectively, life can then become a ridiculous farce, for such a person is completely engrossed in these compulsive ideas, which never allow him a moment's peace, and because of them he fails to notice his real life-task. At times such perfectionism seems to be an unconsciously sought alibi that enables him to escape more important obligations.

Yet not only pedantic prigs are suffocated by formulas. It can also happen to great revolutionaries, who can become as though possessed by an insane justice. In Camus's *The Just Assassins* the idea of justice receives such a magic-demonic splendor that for its realization blood must run in torrents. The "purity" of the idea demands that all half-measures, all hesitation, all weakness be radically abandoned. Strict adherence to the party line of the system allows no further consideration of ideological divergences. Constantly fresh purges and inquisitions are necessary to construct the ultimate kingdom of justice demanded by perfectionism.

No one is as merciless and inhuman as the perfectionist. Yet, if he persists in his standpoint, he may sooner or later be forced into a demoniacal protest against the world order itself and its Creator. For it will never be possible to realize ultimate justice on this earth; there will always be suffering, injustice, weakness, and compromise. The perfectionist has to refuse such a world and must consistently sacrifice his life for a new order: "Death will be the climax of my protest against a world of tears and blood" says Kaliayev in *The Just Assassins*. The perfectionist becomes the great protester and ultimate refuser; he becomes either a tyrant or a rebel, generally both. It is quite logical that Dostoevski's Ivan in *The Brothers Karamazov* narrates the legend of the Grand Inquisitor, who intends to make the world better than it was created to be and who seeks to force the good upon man, even if "for the greater glory of God" he time and again lets hundreds be burned as heretics. It is the same Ivan who earlier had said that he would refuse his "ticket of admission into heaven," since even innocent little children have to suffer so cruelly in this world. This is rebellion, protest against finite reality and ultimately against its Creator, as Alyosha so rightly says. We meet this rebellion in dozens of forms and nuances. Sometimes it is a loud, blustering protest that wants to tear everything apart, and at other times it is a helpless yet constant "No," like a cry of longing. In between we find every shade and combination of aggression and of inferiority feelings. But, no matter whether we deal with a brutally violent or a meek and impotently smiling rebel, there is always the "No" to reality.

In his inner life the perfectionist is a prime example of the clash of opposites. At one time he dreams that he is locked up in prison, pounding on its walls, or deep at the bottom of a concrete cylinder, and then he flies into the sky's wide expanse in rapid rising helicopters or supersonic jets. Hardly ever does he walk in freedom on the dirty soil of the earth, even in his dreams. When he does, he slips and falls or tries to avoid the dirt. The white garment of his justice and perfection must not be stained, and yet his dreams hold up this garment before him soiled and full of holes. The anxiety felt as he awakens cannot let him laugh at the meaning of his dreams.

Depth psychology has not only discovered and repeatedly pointed out this fact of mutual opposition but, through the principle of enantiodromia, has demonstrated that it is a psychic law of the compulsive neurotic. Of course, the psychology of consciousness and also those with a healthy talent of observation are well aware of this. Long ago Pascal wrote the memorable words: *"Qui veut faire l'ange, risque de faire la bête."* Systematic observation and methodical elaboration led further to the demonstration of the inner, lawful connection of perfectionism and neurosis and, through the law of enantiodromia, pointed out the grave danger of perfectionistic compulsive behavior.

THE IDEA-IMAGE OF THE PERFECTIONIST

The perfectionist cannot come to grips with the whole of reality since it does not conform to his idea of the world, men, and things. There are, however, also other forces that further and intensify perfectionism. Here, too, we can generally observe a disguised need of achievement, in some area an exaggerated idealism which is somehow bound up with stubbornness and righteousness: One feels that he must be outstanding in at least one thing, must make his importance secure. Compensatory mechanisms play a big role in this, depending on how much repression is in the service of the "ideal." Often conspicuous is a naïve childishness in certain areas, which can be in a strange contrast to one's otherwise ordinarily mature intellectual and moral qualities: a certain alienation to the world and life, seen by the perfectionist, however, as a positive quality, as "being untouched by the wicked world," as "a nobility of mind untainted by the ordinary." It becomes immediately clear that such childishness is necessarily anxiety-ridden, which in turn intensifies the compulsive character of the perfectionistic behavior. Thus we are faced with an entanglement that finally grows into a Gordian knot which tightens all the faculties of the individual around a hidden center, endowing it with a tenacious power of perseverance and a dynamic force resisting the mightiest efforts of analysis. This center is the inner idea-image.

We all host such an image from earliest childhood. In fact, we usually suppose that every human being is guided by a dominant image which offers him inner fulfillment. We also know that highly productive individuals, the geniuses, wherever they be, are inspired and motivated in their creative process by such inner images. Why is it that for some this idea-image is a creative motoric impulse or at least a helpful model in which they can confide, while it misleads perfectionists into eccentricities and illusions and for them becomes a constant inquisitor and cause of cantankerous behavior and depressions? Why for them is it a fata morgana that makes them ever more thirsty until they finally die of thirst?

The idea-image of the perfectionist has three qualities that render it unsuitable for a true dominant image. First it takes on the traits of *absolute perfection*, which gives it a captivating and hypnotizing effect, endowing it with impulses and dynamics as if everything were a matter of absolute rectitude or absolute guiltlessness, of the highest spirituality or various other kinds of absolutes. As a consequence, this image seems to belong to the category of the numinous, the divine, where alone there is an absolute completion. True, such a dominant image has a certain justification, since it continually orients man toward final transcendence and so also gives him the Augustinian unrest as innermost core. But it becomes unauthentic and neuroticizing as soon as it transfers its claim to the world of the visible and palpable. This transference process does not happen consciously, by way of the intellect, but unconsciously, by way of the emotions and feelings, and much more frequently than we are inclined to believe. Yet, at the same moment the image loses its actual numinous character and transforms it into one of magic quality: To its almost supraworldly splendor is joined the compulsive component.

The *compulsive character*, the second quality of the perfectionistic idea-image, works like a hypnotic command-machine under whose tyranny the perfectionists moan and groan but which they are addicted to and neither can nor want to escape—the image is too fascinating. The compulsive component also endows the image with a rigid, inflexible, static character, fixing and paralyzing the perfectionist so that the flow of his psychic energies comes to a halt. He can no longer adjust to the limiting facts of the human situation, his developmental energies are blocked, which also explains his fear of everything new, unexpected, and unforeseen. Nothing is allowed to entice him out of the tightly bracketed, narrow picture frame of his image. He is identified with his idea-image. What characterizes the "normal individual," however, and especially those who have creative capacities in a certain area is not merely the inner "vision" to be realized but the great fluidity of their creative powers. They, too, desire completion and perfection in their work, but they consider themselves always as beginners constantly carrying out the Sisyphean task of rolling the stone uphill—while the perfectionist wants to be at the end immediately and radically shortens, mutilates, bends, and forces everything that does not fit into the Procrustean bed of his rigid idea. (Our use of the well-known legends of Sisyphus and Procrustes is quite deliberate, since we wish to point up how much these psychic facts are connected with the age-old experiences and insights of mankind.) The rigidity of the perfectionist forces him to seek to ignore the thousand painful steps that must be taken for the realization of true values or else in his "idealism" to leap over them. He wants to be already at the end without honestly and truly going the way with its many phases and stages, its necessary bypasses and side streets.

This rigid attitude of compulsion alienates the perfectionist from life and, at least in this respect, makes him seem infantile. Infantile *alienation to life* is the third characteristic of the perfectionistic idea-image. The tyranny of the dictate of perfection keeps the perfectionist from dealing soberly and realistically with imperfect man and the inadequacies of events. "All or nothing" is his secret motto. In some hidden recess of his being or even in his innermost core (core-neurosis) the perfectionist has stopped short with the child's magic world of phantasy. He wants the absolutely perfect, and it always happens that for him the *best* turns into the enemy of the *good*. Since the idea-image stems from earliest childhood, it grows together with the individual, with his entire feeling, imagining, thinking, sensing, and wanting. It is fixed with a thousand clamps. True, this dominant and ruling image of life goes through many corrections because of failures in professional, family, and married life. It is often questioned, and the individual of relatively good psychic health differentiates this image in the course of all his experiences and disappointments. But the perfectionist stubbornly holds on to it, defends it with entirely childish naïveté and with an almost childish obstinacy tries to make it accepted. Only then is he so sheltered and knows himself so pleasantly "at home" that he is at the end of all his desires. Usually, too, he expects to reach this end without major personal effort, without risk, and without long years of endeavor, for he believes in the magic of his childish obstinate will. Yet time and again he finds himself thrown out of his paradise of shelteredness, and time and again he is told that he must furrow the hard soil of reality "in the sweat of his brow."

Depth psychology is aware of these ideals of the neurotic perfectionist. They are expressed in many symbols, above all in the symbol of the maternal womb, the child's safe nesting place. Perhaps the perfectionist was never allowed to truly experience this shelteredness in his childhood, which could be why his unfulfilled desire for it has taken on such dimensions; or else he may have experienced this pleasant situation beyond all due proportions and remained so long fixed in his state of being spoiled that he shirks from and fears every breath of the "hostile" world. Yet how does such an almost passive-egotistic-sensitive attitude jibe with the exhausting overdemands the perfectionist makes on himself and others? Is this not completely contradictory? But let us not be deceived: The perfectionist makes these exaggerated demands on himself and others only when his illusory image of the world and of men forces them out compulsively, which is the very reason why afterwards he himself suffers from his own overdemand! His heroism is only apparent, for it does not originate in a great inner freedom. Therefore this behavior in no way liberates him, for even in his "great decisions" he is one who is driven, a compulsive neurotic who neither possesses nor wants to possess his freedom: Compulsion is freedom from freedom.[2]

[2] Cf. p. 68, n. 6.

Perfection, absoluteness, paradisaic protectedness: these traits of the perfectionistic idea-image point toward that ultimate position where highest fulfillment and divine perfection rule. Sooner or later, therefore, perfectionism turns into a religious problem. In fact, the perfectionistic neurotic generally is affected by the problem of religion and suffers because of it. The question of his relationship to God gives him no rest and the authenticity or unauthenticity of his piety can grow into his most tormenting problem of life.

Before going further into this particular aspect of perfectionism, it might be worthwhile to refer to the genesis of the perfectionistic idea-image. Everything we have said about this image agrees with what Freud stated concerning the "superego." Yet, in regard to the superego, we know that to a great degree it is the result of very early childhood training. Much well-intended instruction, admonition, and, especially, the living example of parents and teachers have in the course of many years constructed this image of the superego. Therefore it has grown up together with the individual and has become imbedded in his psyche. That is why it is so difficult later on to adjust it to reality. How can one reverse, so to speak, two decades of his life? Therapy has taught us that one can successfully confront such an idea-image only with another, stronger image (never merely with words!) that is rooted even more deeply and, most important, more essentially in the soul. Only the archetypal primordial images, which, in the sense of Jung, are given together with the structure of the soul, have the power to bring the one-sided, distorted caricatures of the superego into their correct form and natural proportions. These structure-given archetypes have generally received their best and most valid form in religious symbols. Thus, once more it becomes necessary to consider the problem of neurotic perfectionism also in its relationship to piety.

PERFECTIONISM AND PIETY

God is the mightiest reality, the suprareality, the fullness of life. Through him all realms of reality, without exception, have their power of existence; they are his resplendence, his reflection. Through him the whole of reality receives its supreme value and its significant meaning. How is it at all possible, then, that some pious people disregard reality and allow it to be reduced and shrunk to miserable little remnants? Why do they let their emotional life wither away, so that they see and experience only the inadequacies of created being? Is it that a certain religiosity (certainly not religion) cultivates perfectionism into luxuriant growth? Does it, perhaps, sink an image into the soul which, through its excessive value and absolute perfection, awakens in man such a longing for the absolute that nothing is any longer sufficient to quench this thirst except the One, the Divine?

In fact, as the history of mysticism shows, the experience of God can be so overwhelming and so deeply seize the whole man, so stir his feelings and fill his heart with such great happiness and joy that in comparison all other experiences of nature, art, love seem inane and dissolve as into nothingness. Those who experience such heights are the great fulfilled ones, the lovers of God; yet, because of this very experience, they must regularly and repeatedly return to the "little" things and find in them an afterglow of their primal experience. They are able to see and experience "God in all things," be it in giving kindness or in merciful compassion, but it always comes from the wide-openness of their God-filled hearts. Those who live and experience in this way are not perfectionists; they are not offended by imperfections and the all too human qualities of people but love humanity in all its weakness and woefulness.

Our perfectionist friends, however, know only the almighty God of their reason: the Absolute. They possess only an abstracted image of his greatness and are afraid of it; they do not experience his all-embracing love for the weak and the small. Their God is a *tremendum* but not at all a *fascinosum*. Almost by necessity they are broken into fragments. This situation causes increased anxiety and lays the foundation of their compulsion-system. In some this consists in a ritual of prayers and pious exercises that demands a constant concern with minutiae. They impose on themselves a pedantically rigid sequence of prayers and good deeds, the fulfillment of which becomes their life's purpose. This ritual is the thing that counts; the person cannot free himself from its hypnotic effect, as it continues to enhance its psychic terrorism and unremittingly increases the number of rituals or at least demands an ever growing intensity in their performance, a more and more perfect playing of the rules.[3] The perfectionist thus turns into a ritualist who, from the very start, so sets up his ritual or so interprets it that it can never be completely carried out with any actual, true, and experiential meaning.

The result of this impossible striving is a psychic disorientation and a state of mind that is a combination of guilt feelings, anxiety, and always new compulsive urges. The formal fulfillment of ritual has replaced the love of God; the means have gradually become an end in themselves. Of course, there are also some simple faithful who give God his due by way of such compulsions, but ordinarily it takes them a long time to feel the pain, since religion for them is primarily a matter of church-going and hardly touches the central and vital problems of real life. But the others, who are incapable of splitting themselves into separate halves, suffer the misery of their compulsive ritual.

The compulsion system can also be the moral system for "the pious." What we had to say about the perfectionist in general, namely that often he cannot find a right relationship to his body and wants to be counted among the guiltless pure or raises his idols to absolute rectitude—all this is intensified under the banner of religion. Then, from the depths of a soul in torment or from the heights of pride comes the dictate: Be perfect "as your heavenly Father is perfect." But strangely enough, it has never happened that such a patient could tell me where this statement is to be found in the gospel or give

[3] Cf. Bernhard Welte, *Vom Wesen und Unwesen der Religion* (Frankfurt: J. Knecht, 1952).

any idea of its meaning in context. But the core is in the context! Matthew in 5:43–48 speaks of "your Father in heaven, who makes his sun to rise on the good and the evil and sends rain on the just and the unjust." He goes on to conclude with the following: "For if you love those that love you, what reward shall you have? Do not even the publicans do that? And if you salute your brethren only, what are you doing more than others? Do not even the gentiles do that? You, therefore, are to be perfect, even as your heavenly Father is perfect." There is no trace of perfectionism here, nothing about absolute justice and purity, nothing about freedom from sin as understood by the perfectionist; only love of enemy and tolerance, understanding openness, and kindness even toward the "evil" and the "unjust."

It might at first seem surprising, but under closer consideration it becomes fully justified and logical that in speaking about perfection Holy Scripture at the same time mentions the one effective means of avoiding all perfectionism: openness and greatness of heart, true love. Without exaggeration we can say that depth psychology's widening of the intrapsychic realm has increased the capacity for and inclination toward this love;[4] many misunderstandings have been avoided or at least corrected as a result of the insights of depth psychology. The attitude of the perfectionist with its moralizing tendency misleads him into an ascetic dilettantism, which in turn neglects the basic demands of the human structure. The

[4] Cf. Gustav Vogel, *Tiefenpsychologie und Nächstenliebe* (Mainz: Matthias Grünewald, 1957).

perfectionist wants to achieve something by force without having a clear insight into the intrapsychic compensatory processes of the instinctual life and without sufficient knowledge as to how a true renunciation and a true sublimation can be at least partially realized. He wants to force himself to do something that ultimately can only be the work of grace.

This compulsive attitude explains how the aim of ascesis can be distorted so that, instead of a right order between body and soul, an unenlightened "mortification" of the body can become a kind of end in itself. That such an attitude stunts and emasculates the Christian image of man seems hardly to touch the skin of consciousness. Temptations are flipped away with a skillful jujitsu of the will, emotions repressed, soul-needs ignored. Reach the high plateau of the "purely spiritual" life! Yet the results of such ascetic bungling, despite the "good intention," are not much better than the assembly-line statues which pockmark our churches in the name of "art" and altogether bloodlessly, soullessly, spiritlessly portray the unauthenticity and unreality of the ideal.

A right order of body and soul presupposes that each of the two layers is tuned to the other so that their sensitive interplay becomes possible in the living product. In this question we agree with Goldbrunner when he says that today the time has come for an ascesis that is body-loving instead of body-hating. The energies of the body should not be repressed but cultivated. One should let himself be carried by the "brother ass" instead of constantly kicking him in the behind.[5] Friendship between spirit and body is important, for the Christian goal of life is not spiritualization (as in certain gnostic groups) but a life-formation which, since Christ's incarnation, sees and understands the value of the body in a completely new light and senses that the body is destined to the same resurrection and glory as the spirit. We admit that in certain cases God has most graciously substituted for the lack of aptitudes and capabilities (we call to mind, for instance, the holy pastor of Ars), and yet we must not presumptuously count on this help. Imprudent expectations and hopes, however, are not infrequently cultivated by perfectionistic groups as virtue-meeting specifications.

In a similar way the completely fresh attitude of the gospel toward sin should be brought to realization. The statement "the greatest of evil is sin" (Schiller) is justified in Christianity only in so far as unbelief also is seen as sin. In all other instances, however, it must be emphasized that Christ did not come for the just and the healthy but for the sinner and the sick and that only those who honestly believe themselves to be such and admit it receive any invitation to the great "wedding feast." The actual struggle of the gospel is directed on the one side against unbelief and on the other side against the very perfectionists who at that time appeared in the garb of the pharisees as "the just ones," although they, too, fell victim to compulsive ideas and mechanisms in the manner of perfectionists of all varieties and

---

[5] Cf. Josef Goldbrunner, *Holiness Is Wholeness* (Notre Dame, Ind.: University of Notre Dame Press, 1964).

times. The gospel judges men more realistically and, by this alone, also truly mercifully: It sees the granite block of sin on the road of man's life and knows that it does not help to stand around in a crowd and stare at it or to pile more stones in front of it in order to hide it, since this only makes it harder to roll out of the way. Perfectionism reveals itself as a compulsive system behind which anxiety always necessarily lurks. Religious perfectionism, too, is anxiety-ridden and therefore diametrically opposed to the Christian religion of love. "There is no fear in love" (1 John 4:18). One should not be too surprised that psychoanalysis took up the mistaken opinion that religious belief is merely an outwardly defensive function of the ego, an assuaging of fear. Thus psychoanalysis failed to reach the religious core, since the neurotic as perfectionist is full of irrational fear also in his religious life. But hidden behind the fear is an image of man which in most cases is the copy of a neuroticized God-image.

All therapy of neurotic perfectionism should be aware that it is a matter of transplanting into life an undwarfed, integral image of man, consisting of spirit and instinct, of conscious and unconscious, and helping the love that is "from God" (1 John 4:7) to break through. It is not a matter of a taking seriously the whole of reality, but of a *doing* seriously. For only he who "does the truth, comes to the light" (John 3:21).

CHAPTER XI

Reflections on Prayer Life

Psychology as science has been concerned with prayer, at least indirectly, for quite a few decades. The psychological laboratory of the twenties dealt especially with the "psychic construct of religious experience,"[1] and prayers and religious texts served as the pattern and stimuli of these experiences. But the extensive works of Rudolf Otto, Werner Gruehn, Georg Wunderle, and in part that of Alois Mager should also be mentioned as laying the foundation for research on prayer.[2]

Today's psychology has a different approach to the phenomenon of prayer life. More academic investigation of the various functions and their interplay in prayer has given way to the existentially alarming questions of authenticity and of the transcendent power of prayer. This view of the problem is intimately connected with the wide breakthrough of depth psychology, which first

[1] Karl Girgensohn, *Der seelische Aufbau des religiösen Erlebens* (1930).
[2] Rudolf Otto, *The Idea of the Holy* (London and New York: Oxford University Press, 1923); Werner Gruehn, *Religionpsychologie* (1926); Georg Wunderle, *Das Irrationale im religiösen Erleben*.

229

as an unmasking psychology most saliently articulated the problem of authenticity and then, seeing the soul as a closed energy-field, had also to formulate the question of the openness of prayer toward a suprapsychic world in order to finally deal more and more, as analysis of existence (in some form), with the authenticity of man and his natural powers awaiting realization. Thus we face, on the one hand, subjective and individual problems for whose solution final and objective standards can hardly be found—and, on the other hand, an objective question based on the nature of man, a question apparently age-old yet formulated with new intensity out of a new situation.

I THE PROBLEM OF AUTHENTICITY

Strangely enough, it was not an analytic psychologist who coined the alarmingly realistic phrase "*omnis homo mendax.*" Yet we can say that there is no expression of human activity in which this bold and yet so profoundly true observation of the psalmist is more valid than when man approaches God in prayer. To overcome a final and imperceptible unauthenticity in this central action of man a gift of God himself seems necessary and one which, according to the testimony of the greats of Christianity, is given only very late. Still there are many adult Christians who sense, indefinitely but clearly, something of this unauthenticity and suffer from it. Timidly and regretfully they tell themselves and others that they "cannot pray right," referring not only to the almost chronic fruitlessness of their prayer—which has still not made them more resigned, more mature and kind—but also to their lack of inner contact with the Being who is, after all, the object of their prayerful concentration. They may even sense that this kind of prayer is indicative of a spiritual deficiency, which they would almost like to hide from themselves and others. It is as if the "not being able to pray right" has become an incessant secret accuser of their own ego, even though this ego does not actually feel very guilty, since it is more a felt premonition than a clear knowing. But because one realizes he is not alone in this reaction and that nearly all his friends and acquaintances have the same feeling, he puts up with it as something unavoidable and unalterable.

Yet it could be so constructive if he would try to investigate this spiritual deficiency as the source of unauthenticity and find out a little more about it. A starting point for this investigation might be the well-known definition of prayer: "elevation of the heart." What, from the psychological viewpoint, is this "heart" that is elevated to God? A conscious reflection may perhaps bring new clarity into this somehow dusty concept of heart and contribute to the solution of the problem of prayer.

The designation of prayer as a function of the heart is a masterwork of healthy instinct, although the heart can hardly be referred to as a psychic mechanism. But is it not typical of symbolical thinking to say the right thing even without full awareness? The heart is the symbol for that inner center of man which encompasses his being as a whole and incorporates and represents it as a unity.

It is primarily a matter of the wholeness of the psychic function-apparatus. All specific functions—from the dynamic of the instincts, the instinct of self-preservation, and the libidinal drives of completion and union, up to the power of imagination; from the temperament, and experiential and perceptual knowledge, up to the acts of will and the lasting and deeply rooted feelings—come together, as through a convergent lens, in what we call the heart. Here they converge into a single whole, as though in a crystallization point, so that it can be difficult to distinguish their individual functions. In this center they work hand in hand so unitedly that intellect and feelings do not go their separate ways or strive for contradictory objects. The wholeness and unity of the psychic functional structure is, in the "heart," lived as experience and felt as a strength and harmony. Wherever the heart truly is and is felt as the symbol of such wholeness and unity, there is no psychic fragmentation, no splitting. Psychic dissociation, one of the most important backgrounds of neurotic diseases, does not appear. Whatever originates in and rises from the heart is never an outpouring of fleeting, half-true feelings, nor the conclusion of a bloodless intellect, nor a violent stream of power-pumped knowledge, nor the product of a foot-loose, spendthrift phantasy; it is the unbroken primal power and fully rounded figure of the soul which—neither in a post-synthesis nor in any painful putting together of parts but in the spontaneous fullness of its nature—manifests itself as wide-openness through its concentrated inner closedness.

What makes prayer so difficult for man—not only today but perhaps now more than before—is that he does not yet possess his heart; he hasn't quite "made it;" he is not yet himself. He lacks this innermost psychic center. Thus the problem of prayer is the problem of a fragmented humanity. By this we do not mean chiefly a fragmentation in the outside world (*Flight from God*, as Picard masterly described it), but we refer to the inner escapes, the many hundreds of paths of the psychic labyrinth. Inner fragmentation, this halfway-ness or one-sidedness, makes prayer unauthentic. It makes the intellect argue against religious feelings emerging from the primal depth, makes phantasy a stubborn night bird that tries to fly by day, wildly fluttering and bumping its head against the walls of social realities. It makes will power often behave like a blind and violent bull that charges after a real or imagined piece of red cloth—as, for instance, one's own sensuality and sexuality—until it is exhausted. The "loss of the center" is first and foremost an intrapsychic condition that banishes man to the periphery of his own being, causing him to run around ecstatically in the *circulus vitiosus* of his many desires, addictions, and inanities and of his seemingly ideal perfectionistic striving. Then, add to this a vague feeling of guilt which in most cases is not resolved into a clear and convincing consciousness of guilt and the result is an even greater inner insecurity, anxiety, and fragmentation. How can such an individual so pray that today's call to God will still be valid tomorrow? He sees his own situation constantly shifting, according to that point on the periphery where he happens to be. Thus his prayer must seem to him somehow unauthentic. It is not the clearly oriented heart-flow of his existence but only the valve of a psychic function that happens to be under pressure. This at least semiconscious unauthenticity makes one experience prayer as questionable, and one adopts an increasingly diffident attitude toward it, both in regard to himself and to others.

If prayer is to become a true expression of full and whole humanness, of the heart of man, such humanness must, first, again be possible. True, there are always some who have either preserved or have once more achieved a good inner integration of their being; but there is still the problem of the many who, because of their psychic disintegration, cannot express themselves with relative authenticity and therefore even in their relationship with God suffer from the unauthenticity of their prayer. It is easy enough to see that in this situation neither can liturgical prayer be of any deep-reaching and lasting help, since a true community cannot grow out of a collection of disintegrated and psychically dissociated individuals.

Thus there actually remain but two forms of prayer experienced as authentic. The most convincing form is the prayer of "fragmentation" itself, in which a secure formulation is no longer tried, no theologically founded train of thought forged into articles of faith, but only the outcry of the heart is uttered, or a mute gesture of resignation is given without any pretense of a performance of religious value. Here prayer takes on the seal of authenticity, since it does not come out of an incidental mood of the moment but is the expression of a person-molding, existential need.

Equally convincing to some is the "secularized" form of prayer, which is quite suspect to austere religious groups as being only "natural piety." We know that today many are fleeing into nature not only from the stone walls of the city but from the stone walls of the churches. They flee from an artificial world of modern technology and hectic busyness. They find it embarrassing to find a similar busyness even in the church. A non-Catholic recently told me that he attended Sunday Mass in a very large city and was dismayed to find there was not a moment of quiet, in fact no possibility of a single minute of concentration. Individuals with a sensitive, perhaps oversensitive, sensorium for authenticity will time and again revolt against this organized piety and its conventionally mechanized forms. They reject "this whole system of worshipping God as disgusting" (van Gogh) and try to find the Almighty in the simple but original realm of nature. They flee from their own psychic fragmentation into the healthiness and wholeness of nature.

This is picture enough of one of man's problems in regard to prayer. It may give an insight into the terrible struggle of some individuals for an authentic confrontation with God and put into perspective the sincerity of this struggle.

II TRANSCENDENCE OR PROJECTION?

The person who prays, especially if he is sincere, faces another problem which is no less disturbing and perhaps even a pain without relief: "Am I really talking to God? Have I actually broken through the thick wall that separates Creator and creature?" Or does the praying man only build a thicker wall and in his prayer become more aware of its impenetrability? Does he ever talk to anyone outside himself? Is prayer any more than a conversation with one's own better ego—the innermost "self" that ought to be? One begins to suspect that prayer is merely an intense concentration on the highest numinous intrapsychic "archetype," on intrapsychic images, so that one begins to understand Rilke: "We have built images in front of you like walls, / And yes, already a thousand walls stand round you." This suspicion can so grow that we are in continual torment wondering whether prayer is really merely a function of our own mechanism of projection, which is so common in our daily interpersonal relationships, especially when emotion and affect tend to upstage us. Is prayer, then, basically a projection of subjective psychic images and inherent ideas and emotions onto a mental fiction or onto a real yet unknown being?

Needless to say, the "healthy" average individual seldom entertains so much suspicion. The unreflecting, spontaneous, and especially the extroverted type requires a long time even to come to a hint of this kind of thinking. He soon learns to believe in the reality of his confrontation with God or else will give up prayer as something odd and indigestible. It is only later that he, too, must face up to the problem, when he tries repeatedly to get closer to the invisible God who is so intangibly distant. The critical thinking, introverted type, however, is generally thrown earlier into this desert solitude. He also becomes more quickly aware of his psychic "projections" in other human relationships and then experiences that his Thou-relationships are caused and supported more or less intensively by his own positive or negative psychic images, by a kind of fata morgana. And finally prayer becomes for him also an unbearable monologue which never receives an answer from "above."

Although we are convinced that this represents one of the most central problems of the psychology of religion we cannot here go into further detail. The absolute transcendence of God seems to be an inaccessible frontier which even mystical encounters with God cannot completely cross, since even these ways of encounter happen by means of extremely powerful images (the light, or the sun-wheel, or "secret words" [2 Cor. 12:4]). No matter how overwhelming and strong the impression of directness may be, no matter how primordially it may grasp the person, stir and shake him, a more precise analysis makes it immediately evident that it is still only an indirect experience of God, which, as a very sudden and short-cut final process, as an ascent from the created to the non-created, is always overwhelming but, nonetheless, can never be a leap into the absolute. Here John is so right: "No one has at any time seen God" (John 1:18).

Thus for the person of insight his most personal act is at one and the same time his hardest test. Every endeavor to come nearer to God remains somehow an illusion. The absolute distance cannot be gradually reduced. Prayer no longer seems to be a "way" to God which one can follow faithfully and courageously. The indiscreet intensity of certain prayer forms can, especially to those outside the

Church, seem rather naïve and even neurotic. Did not Christ himself say: "But in praying, do not multiply words, as the Gentiles do" (Matt. 6:7). Of what value are those wordy, baroque prayer tirades by which one tries to "storm" God and heaven? What good are all the stereotyped phrases behind which a psychologist can clearly observe the compulsive repetitions of an anxiety neurosis or a dry and shallow soullessness? In fact, can this prayer still be called a dialogue with God, a close communication of soul with soul?

Such an experience can lead to two temptations: One might begin to adopt a more and more indifferent attitude toward God. Since all prayer is like an arrow that falls short a great distance from its goal, what good is the constant bending of the bow? What good the restless running along this spiral which has its center in the infiniteness of eternal distance? A great lethargy overcomes the isolated and lonesome pray-er, vexation in the face of his many futile attempts. Acedia and melancholy are not diseases restricted to medieval monks. Or the person may try another way: He lapses into a deep awful silence before the Eternal. A prayer of silence and quiet seems the best possible attitude; words are too noisy, too presumptuous, inadequate; they sound hollow, empty and, above all, superfluous when spoken to him who in his omniscience already knows everything perfectly. It seems better to wait in inner stillness and patience until the silent God himself speaks the first word to the soul. Pascal, at the end of his life, withdrew into this silence and became completely dumb, overwhelmed by the inner recognition of the infinite distance that separated him from the Eternal One.

On the psychological plane no solution can be found for the problem of projection and transcendence. This problem points to the sphere of faith and to the validity of other categories, where another, new spirit prays within man and through man, a spirit which as "Holy Spirit" already reaches into the depths of divinity. Only out of this "dwelling" of the Spirit is it possible to develop the inner attitude of reverence for God that becomes a life in the "presence of God," so that now one "prays without ceasing." Yet, this essential attitude of prayer also remains an activity of faith, and from the biblical viewpoint our existence continues to be a waiting for the revelation of the sonship of God, for full and real participation in the divine streams of life. Prayer is a basic function of this faith and this waiting. It is always as strong and close to God as the faith supporting it.

But does not faith necessarily withdraw from all psychological interference? We know that the preamble of the "analysis fidei" reserved a place even for the natural dispositions in respect to the capacity for and openness to faith. Although intellectual deliberations and insights belong preeminently to these dispositions, we should not overlook or underestimate the archetypal soul images deeply rooted in the structure of our nature. The fact that we cannot here and now know and love the Eternal One "face to face," that our knowing is "through a mirror in an obscure manner" (1 Cor. 13:12), does not mean that it makes no difference what kind of images and symbols lead to the realization of this ultimate know-ing. There are also neuroticized God-images and God-concepts, which are not only very inadequate but even distorted and repulsive, in as much as they are based either on a single dogma in complete disregard of the polarizing statements of Holy Scripture, or else lopsidedly represent a moralizing bookkeeper God, a fussy, revenge-ful and touchy God of the law.[3] Prayer nourished by such inner ideas is almost by necessity inhibited and unfree and characterized by anxiety- and compulsive neurosis.

Thus it is of utmost importance that the archetypal God-image lying in the deepest ground of our soul be connected with consciousness. He created man "accord-ing to his own image and likeness." Perhaps the most valuable contribution of Jung's depth psychology is its untiring effort to build a bridge between the upper psy-chic layers and the structure-given ground-roots. The re-awakened understanding of the great primordial symbols, gestures, and sounds of our soul, the heritage of all peo-ples and cultures, helps in giving these dynamic domi-nant images of earthly being new impetus toward the formation of our human existence and therefore toward more integral, authentic, and psychically more productive activities and ways of life. Our prayer life, too, will profit from this, since the natural dispostions, unique to each individual, offer it a favorable or less favorable *potentia oboedientialis.* Pope Pius XII, in his address to the Fifth International Congress of Psychotherapy and Clinical Psychology, April 13, 1953, rightly emphasized the signifi-

[3] Cf. Chapter VIII, "The Neuroticized God-Image."

cance of the psychic dynamisms investigated by depth psychology, which cause the soul to gravitate upward and thus are a confirmation of Augustine's statement, *"Inquietum est cor nostrum, donec requiescat in Te."*

After such reflections one is tempted to point out the ambivalence of all human activity—and that of prayer in particular. As long as this activity is seen as a psychic phenomenon, it will always remain somehow ambivalent. It seems to be an inorganic foreign body which, because of its unauthentic and utopian character, one would like to eliminate from a nature that has grown up straight and healthy. Yet it is at the same time the deepest expression of a being that is all need, so much so that even the non-Christian poet must say: "When it comes down to it there are only prayers" (Rilke).

Only if one understands prayer as the expression of an existence which, as a true *ex-istere*, cannot find a solid stand within itself but begins with a "standing-outside" in order to know and realize itself, can one love prayer as a faithful being-in-tension toward him in whom "everything holds together" (Col. 1:17).

INDEX

243